THE ENCHANTED HEART OF
ARIZONA

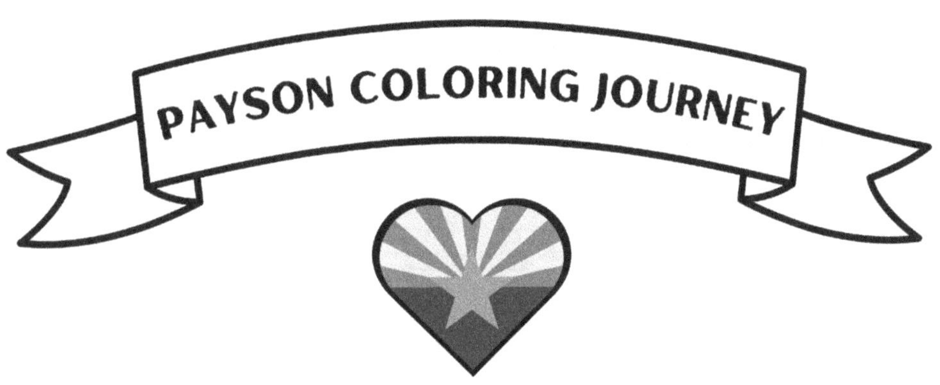

CREATED BY KATHERINE BLUMA
AND JEWEL JOHNSON

The Enchanted Heart of Arizona
Payson Coloring Journey

Authors: Katherine Bluma, Jewel Johnson.
Published by: My Success Strategist
Front and Back Cover by: Jewel Johnson
Illustrations by: Nataliia Savchenko
Copyright © 2024 by My Success Strategist

Disclaimer: This coloring book, "The Enchanted Heart of Arizona: Payson Coloring Journey ," is an independent publication created for entertainment and informational purposes only. The content of this book, including all illustrations and descriptions, is not affiliated with, endorsed by, or officially connected to any of the businesses, wineries, spas, or attractions featured within. All business names, logos, and identifying features are used for illustrative purposes only and remain the property of their respective owners. While every effort has been made to ensure the accuracy of the information presented, the author and publisher do not guarantee the completeness or currency of the content. Readers are advised to verify details directly with the businesses before making any plans or purchases. This book is not intended as a substitute for professional advice or services. The author and publisher disclaim any liability, loss, or risk incurred as a consequence, directly or indirectly, of the use and application of any of the contents of this book.

ABOUT THE CREATORS

Kat Bluma, co-creator of The Enchanted Heart of Arizona, brings a fresh perspective and deep appreciation for her adopted hometown to this charming project. Originally from Milwaukee, Wisconsin, Kat has called Payson home since 2017. Her journey of discovery in this picturesque Arizona town has inspired her to collaborate on a coloring book that invites both locals and visitors to explore Payson's hidden treasures.

Since moving to Payson, Kat has immersed herself in the community, embracing the outdoor lifestyle and uncovering the town's unique character. This coloring book is her way of sharing the wonder and excitement she's experienced while getting to know her new home. Through this project, she aims to showcase Payson's historical sites, community events, local shops, diverse wildlife, scenic hiking trails, and breathtaking natural wonders.

By partnering with Jewel Johnson, she brings together a newcomer's fresh eyes and a longtime resident's deep knowledge, creating a unique exploration of Payson's charm. Kat hopes this coloring book will encourage both residents and visitors to discover the magic of Payson, learn about its rich history, and appreciate the natural beauty that surrounds it.

Jewel Johnson, co-creator of The Enchanted Heart of Arizona, brings her deep love and passion for her hometown to this charming project. Growing up in Payson, Jewel was always involved in community activities and had a profound love for the outdoors. These experiences inspired her to create a coloring book that invites both locals and tourists to explore the town's historical sites, community events, local shops, wildlife, hikes, and natural wonders.

Jewel's connection to Payson is personal and heartfelt. By creating this coloring book, she aims to give back to the town that played such a significant role in her life. She hopes to encourage families and individuals to discover the unique aspects of Payson, learn about its rich history, and appreciate the natural beauty that surrounds it.

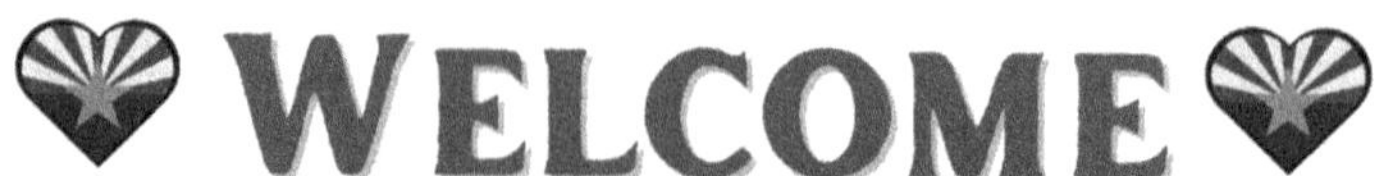

❤ WELCOME ❤

Dear Fellow Explorer and Art Lover!

Welcome to this journey through the heart of Payson and the wonders of Arizona's Rim Country. Creating this coloring book has been an eye-opening adventure, one that has deepened my appreciation for the beauty and richness of our local communities.

As I researched and sketched the subjects for this book, I found myself continually amazed by the natural wonders, historical treasures, and unique character of Payson and its surrounding areas. From the majestic Ponderosa pines of the Mogollon Rim to the charming Swiss Village, each discovery brought with it a new appreciation for the place I call home.

This project has inspired me to venture beyond the familiar confines of larger cities and explore the hidden gems that small towns offer. I've learned that there's an incredible world waiting to be discovered just outside our usual routines - a world of breathtaking landscapes, rich history, and warm, welcoming communities.

Through this process, I've gained a deeper understanding of the importance of supporting local businesses, preserving our natural environments, and celebrating the unique character of each town. I've come to realize that these small communities are the backbone of our state, each with its own stories to tell and wonders to share.

My hope is that as you color these pages and read about the subjects depicted, you'll be inspired to embark on your own journey of discovery. Whether you're a longtime resident of Arizona or a visitor to our beautiful state, I encourage you to seek out the small towns, explore the natural beauty, and immerse yourself in the local culture and history.

Let this book be your starting point for new adventures. Use it as inspiration to plan day trips, weekend getaways, or even longer explorations of Arizona's diverse landscapes and communities. As you do, I hope you'll experience the same sense of wonder and connection that I've found in creating this book.

So, grab your colored pencils, markers, or crayons, and let's begin this colorful journey together. May it open your eyes to the beauty around us and inspire you to support, explore, and celebrate the unique character of Arizona's small towns and natural wonders.

Happy coloring and happy exploring!

THE ENCHANTED HEART OF ARIZONA

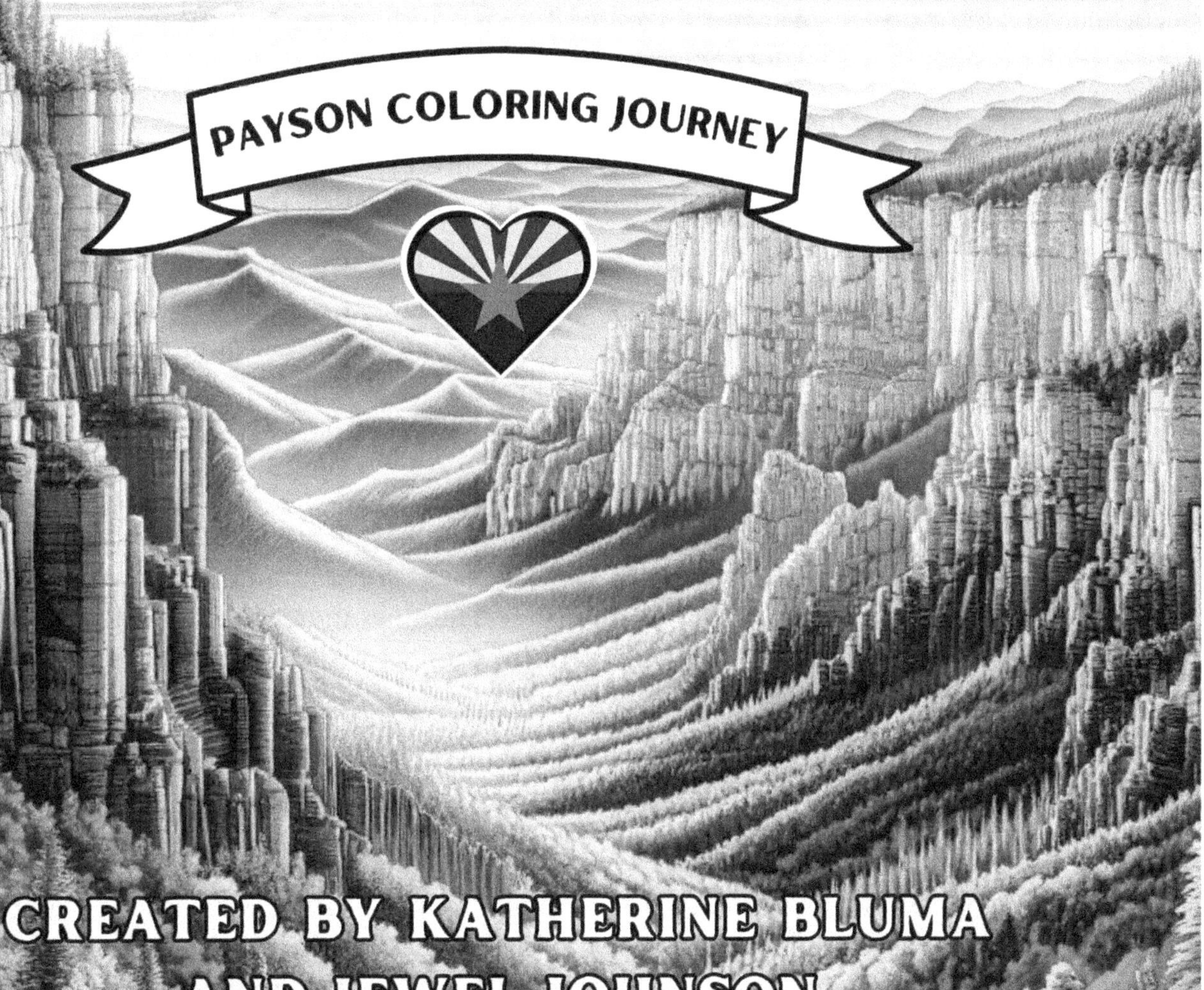

CREATED BY KATHERINE BLUMA AND JEWEL JOHNSON

Payson, Arizona: Where Patriotism and Community Spirit Shine Bright

Nestled in the heart of Arizona's Rim Country, Payson is a town where patriotism runs deep and community spirit thrives. This close-knit community of about 15,000 residents exemplifies the values of small-town America, with a strong sense of pride in both their local heritage and their nation.

Payson's patriotic spirit is evident throughout the year, but it truly comes alive during holidays like Independence Day and Veterans Day. The town's Fourth of July celebration is a highlight, featuring a spectacular fireworks display over the Mogollon Rim, patriotic parades, and community gatherings that bring together residents and visitors alike.

The town's respect for veterans is palpable. The Veterans Memorial, located in Green Valley Park, serves as a poignant tribute to those who have served. Throughout the year, various events honor local veterans, showcasing the community's deep appreciation for their sacrifices.

Fun fact:

The Zane Grey Cabin, a replica of the famous Western author's original retreat, stands as a testament to Payson's commitment to preserving its cultural heritage while fostering a strong sense of community and American values.

Community spirit in Payson goes beyond patriotic displays. It's evident in the way neighbors help each other, in the vibrant local volunteer scene, and in the town's numerous community events. From summer concerts in the park to holiday light parades, there's always something bringing people together.

Local organizations and churches play a significant role in fostering this sense of community. They organize food drives, support local families in need, and create opportunities for residents to connect and contribute to their town's wellbeing.

Payson's schools actively promote civic engagement and patriotism among the younger generation, ensuring that the town's strong community values are passed down and preserved.

Whether it's rallying around a local cause, celebrating national holidays with gusto, or simply enjoying the camaraderie of small-town life, Payson exemplifies the best of American community spirit. It's a place where patriotism isn't just displayed on holidays, but is woven into the fabric of daily life, creating a warm, welcoming atmosphere for all who call Payson home or come to visit.

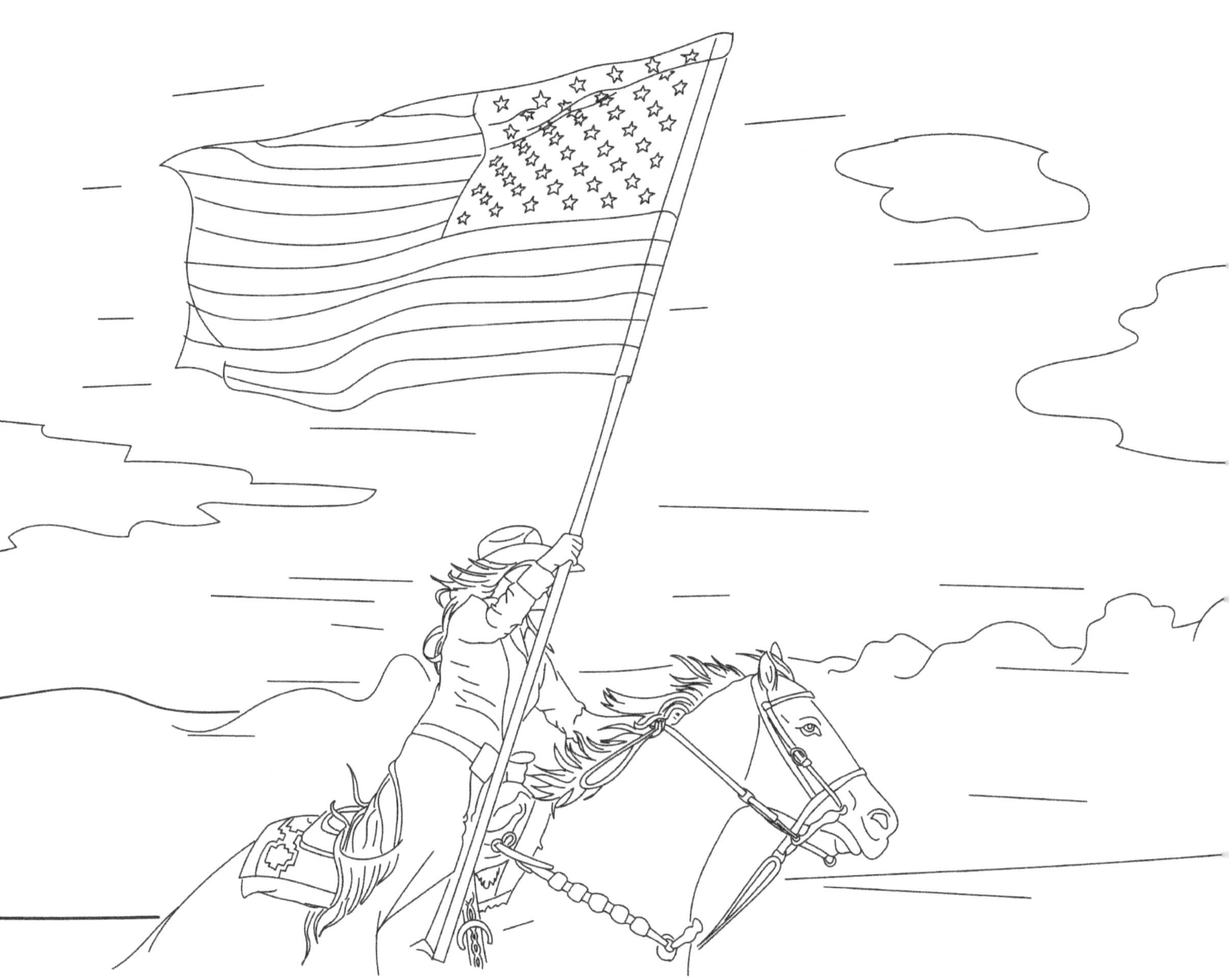

Payson, a picturesque town nestled in Arizona's Rim Country, is home to the World's Oldest Continuous Rodeo. This iconic event has been thrilling spectators since 1884, making it a true piece of living Western history.

The Payson Rodeo, held annually in August, brings together top cowboys and cowgirls from across the country to compete in classic rodeo events. These include bull riding, barrel racing, team roping, and steer wrestling. The dusty arena comes alive with the thunder of hooves, the cheers of the crowd, and the spirit of the Old West.

> ### *Fun fact:*
>
> **The Payson Rodeo began 8 years before the incorporation of Payson itself and 28 years before Arizona became a state! It has run continuously through two World Wars, the Great Depression, and even a global pandemic, earning its title as the "World's Oldest Continuous Rodeo".**

What started as an informal gathering of local ranchers showing off their skills has grown into a major event that draws thousands of visitors to Payson each year. Despite its growth, the rodeo maintains its small-town charm and connection to Arizona's ranching heritage.

This long-standing tradition not only celebrates the skills of modern-day cowboys and cowgirls but also serves as a living link to Arizona's frontier past. It's a colorful reminder of the state's rich Western heritage and the enduring spirit of its people.

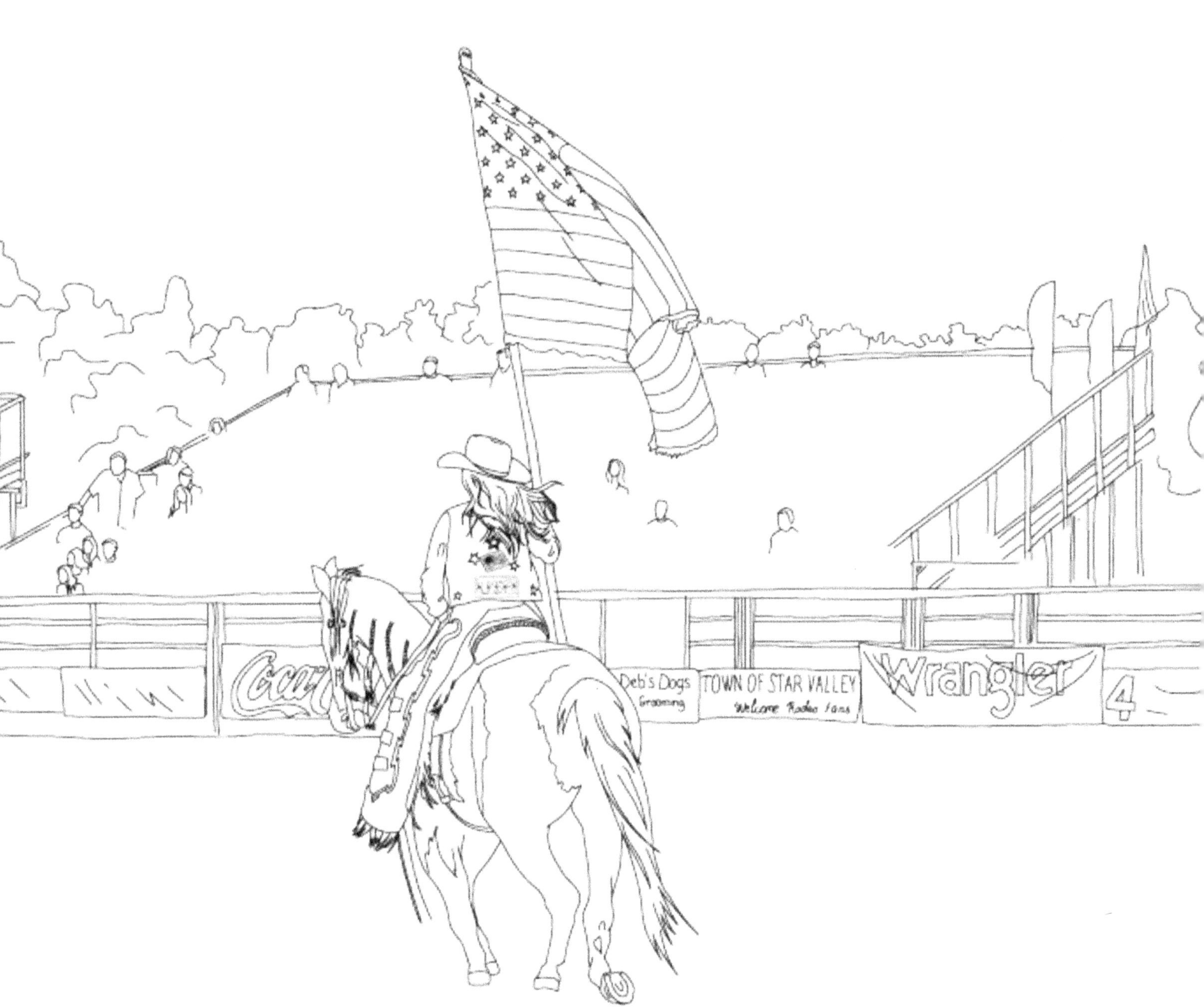

Coca-Cola
Deb's Dogs
Grooming
TOWN OF STAR VALLEY
Welcome Rodeo fans
Wrangler
4

The Payson Rodeo Parade: A Colorful Celebration of Western Heritage

Every August, the streets of Payson come alive with the sights and sounds of the annual Rodeo Parade. This beloved event is a highlight of the World's Oldest Continuous Rodeo, a tradition that has been part of Payson's identity since 1884.

The parade is a vibrant showcase of Payson's rich western heritage and community spirit. Spectators line the streets as a procession of colorful floats, horseback riders, vintage cars, and marching bands make their way through the heart of town. The air is filled with the clip-clop of hooves, the rhythm of music, and the cheers of excited onlookers.

Participants in the parade represent a wide cross-section of the community. Local businesses, schools, community organizations, and rodeo competitors all take part, creating a diverse and lively spectacle. Many parade entries embrace western themes, with riders dressed in their finest cowboy and cowgirl attire.

Fun fact:

The Grand Marshal of the parade is often a person of significance to the community or the rodeo world, adding an element of anticipation to each year's event.

One of the most beloved features of the parade is the horse-drawn wagons and stagecoaches, which transport spectators back to the days of the Old West. These authentic replicas, often beautifully restored, are a testament to Payson's commitment to preserving its frontier history.

The Rodeo Parade is more than just a prelude to the rodeo; it's a community celebration that brings together residents and visitors alike. Families often make a day of it, arriving early to secure the best viewing spots and enjoying the festive atmosphere.

Whether you're watching the skilled equestrians, admiring the creative floats, or simply soaking in the joyful ambiance, the Payson Rodeo Parade offers a delightful glimpse into the heart and spirit of this charming Arizona town. It's a colorful reminder of the enduring appeal of Western culture and the strong sense of community that defines Payson.

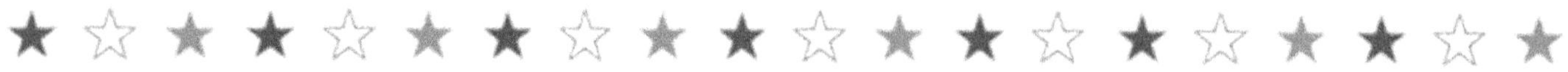

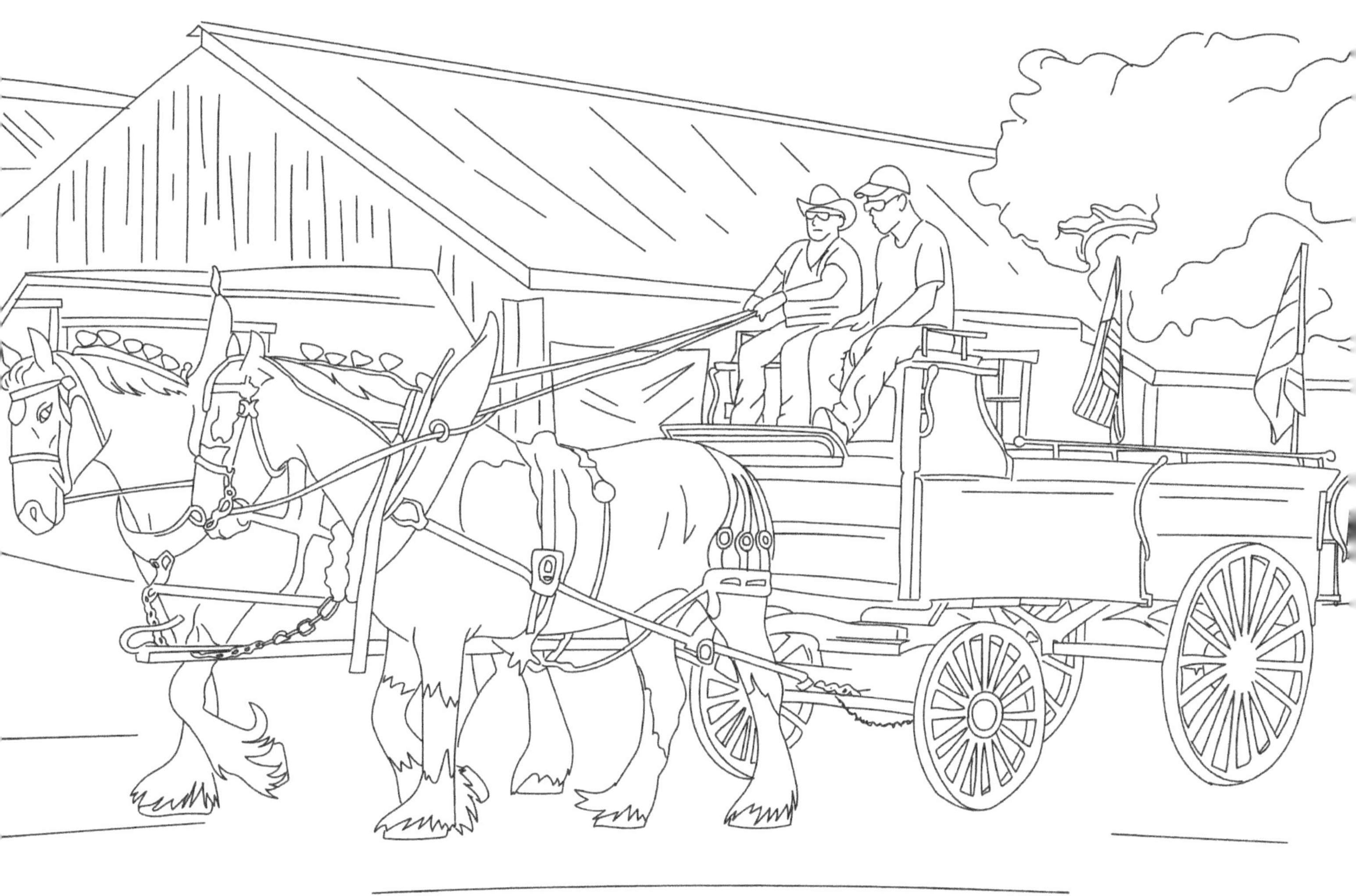

The Role of Steers in the Payson Rodeo: A Test of Cowboy Skill

The Payson Rodeo, known as the "World's Oldest Continuous Rodeo" since 1884, showcases various events that celebrate the skills of cowboys and cowgirls. Among these, events featuring steers play a crucial and exciting role.

Steers, which are castrated male cattle typically between 1-2 years old, are used in several key rodeo events:

1. Steer Wrestling (also known as Bulldogging): In this event, a cowboy chases a steer on horseback, then leaps from his horse to wrestle the steer to the ground. This event tests the cowboy's strength, timing, and agility.

2. Team Roping: Two mounted cowboys work together to rope a steer - one ropes the horns or head (the header), while the other ropes the hind legs (the heeler). This event showcases teamwork and precision.

3. Steer Roping: A single cowboy must rope a steer around the horns, throw the rope over the steer's right hip, and then circle the steer with his horse, bringing it to a stop.

The use of steers in the Payson Rodeo connects modern-day spectators to the practical skills that were essential for working cowboys in Arizona's ranching history. These events demonstrate the techniques that cowboys used (and still use) to manage cattle on the range.

> ### *Fun fact:*
>
> Steers used in rodeos are specifically bred and raised for these events. They're generally larger and more robust than regular cattle, making the competitions more challenging and exciting.

Animal welfare is a top priority in modern rodeos, including Payson's. Steers are handled with care, given regular veterinary check-ups, and are only used for short periods before being returned to pasture.

Whether you're watching the lightning-fast steer wrestling or the precise teamwork of team roping, the steer events at the Payson Rodeo offer thrilling displays of cowboy and cowgirl skills, keeping alive the traditions of Arizona's rich ranching heritage.

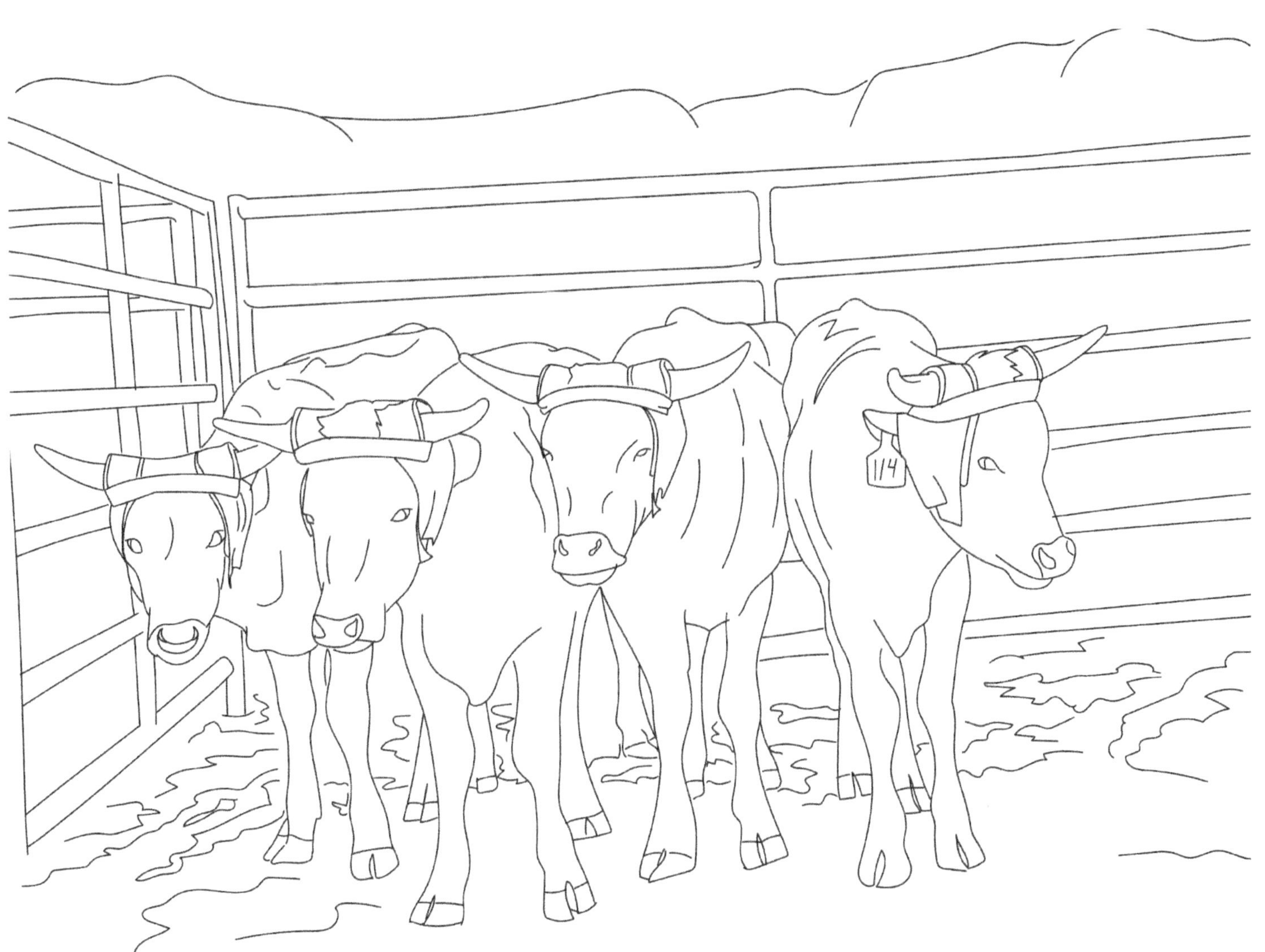

The Hashknife Pony Express is a unique Arizona tradition that brings the Old West to life each January. This annual event recreates the historic mail delivery system of the 1860s, carrying mail on horseback from Holbrook to Scottsdale, Arizona.

Named after the Hashknife Outfit, one of Arizona's historic cattle ranches, this 200-mile journey takes about five days to complete. A group of skilled riders, dressed in authentic cowboy attire, relay special letters and postcards across rugged terrain, battling winter weather and challenging landscapes.

The ride begins in Holbrook, where riders collect mail from the post office. They then set out across Arizona's diverse geography, from high deserts to pine forests, passing through towns like Heber, Payson, and Fountain Hills before reaching their final destination in Scottsdale.

> ### *Fun fact:*
>
> The Hashknife Pony Express is officially sanctioned by the U.S. Postal Service. Each piece of mail carried by the riders receives a special "via Pony Express" postmark, making these letters highly prized by stamp collectors and history enthusiasts alike.

This annual event, which has been running since 1958, is more than just a reenactment. It's a living tribute to Arizona's pioneer spirit and a reminder of the state's rich postal history. The arrival of the Pony Express in Scottsdale is celebrated with a festive parade, allowing spectators to witness a piece of Old West tradition in modern times.

The Hashknife Pony Express serves as a colorful link between Arizona's past and present, keeping the spirit of the frontier alive in the 21st century.

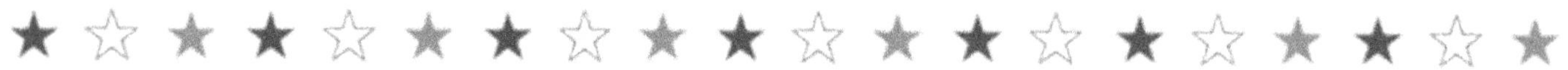

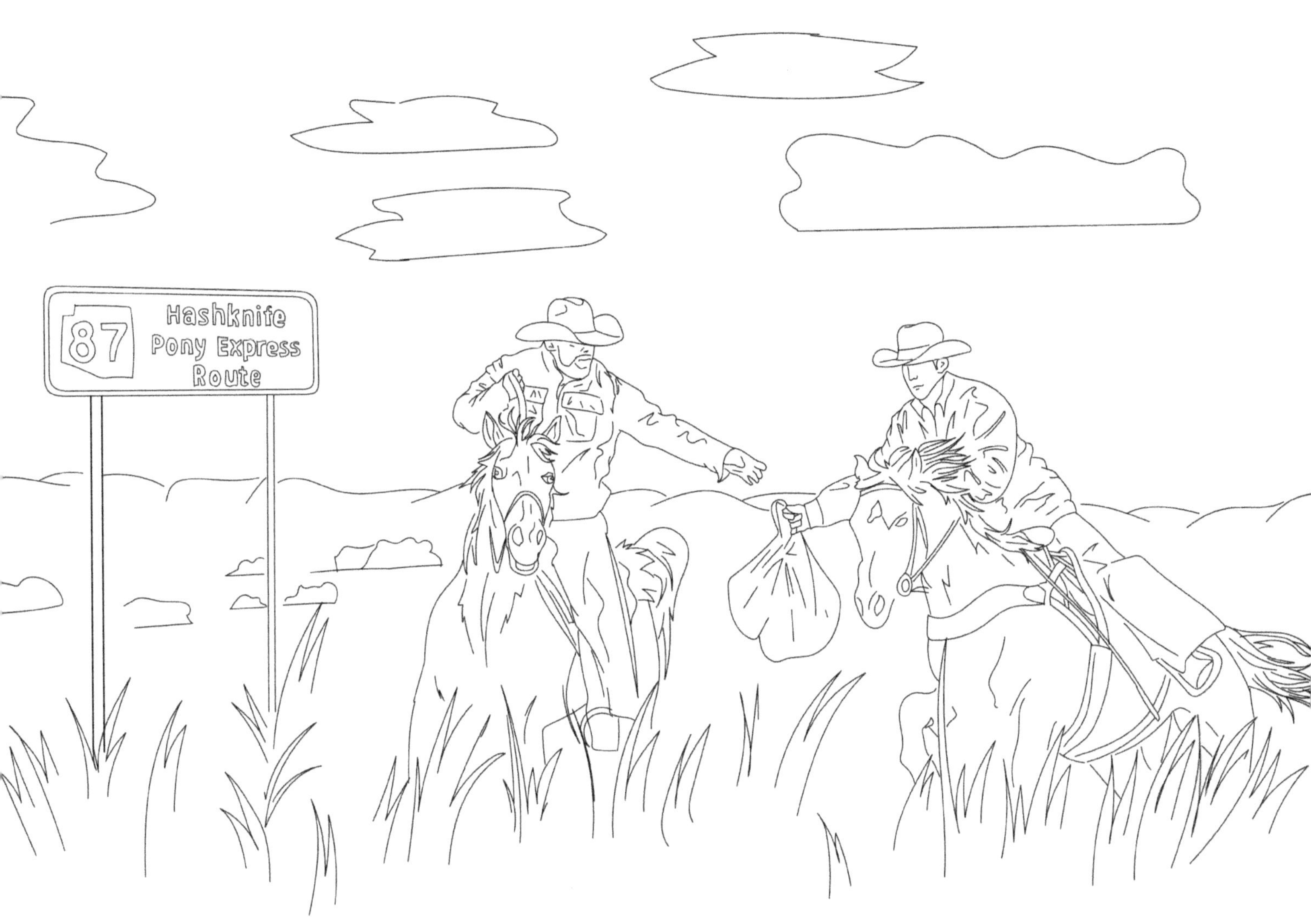

87
Hashknife
Pony Express
Route

General merchandise stores were once the heart of small town life in Arizona. These stores typically offered a wide variety of goods, from groceries and hardware to clothing and household items. In towns like Payson, such stores often served as community hubs, where locals would gather to shop, socialize, and catch up on news.

Many of these stores in Arizona date back to the late 19th or early 20th century, reflecting the town's history and growth.

They often feature historic architecture, with wooden storefronts, large display windows, and interior details like tin ceilings or wooden shelving.

Fun fact:

In many Arizona towns, old general stores have been preserved or restored, offering visitors a glimpse into the past while still serving modern needs. Some continue to operate as stores, while others have been converted into museums or other businesses.

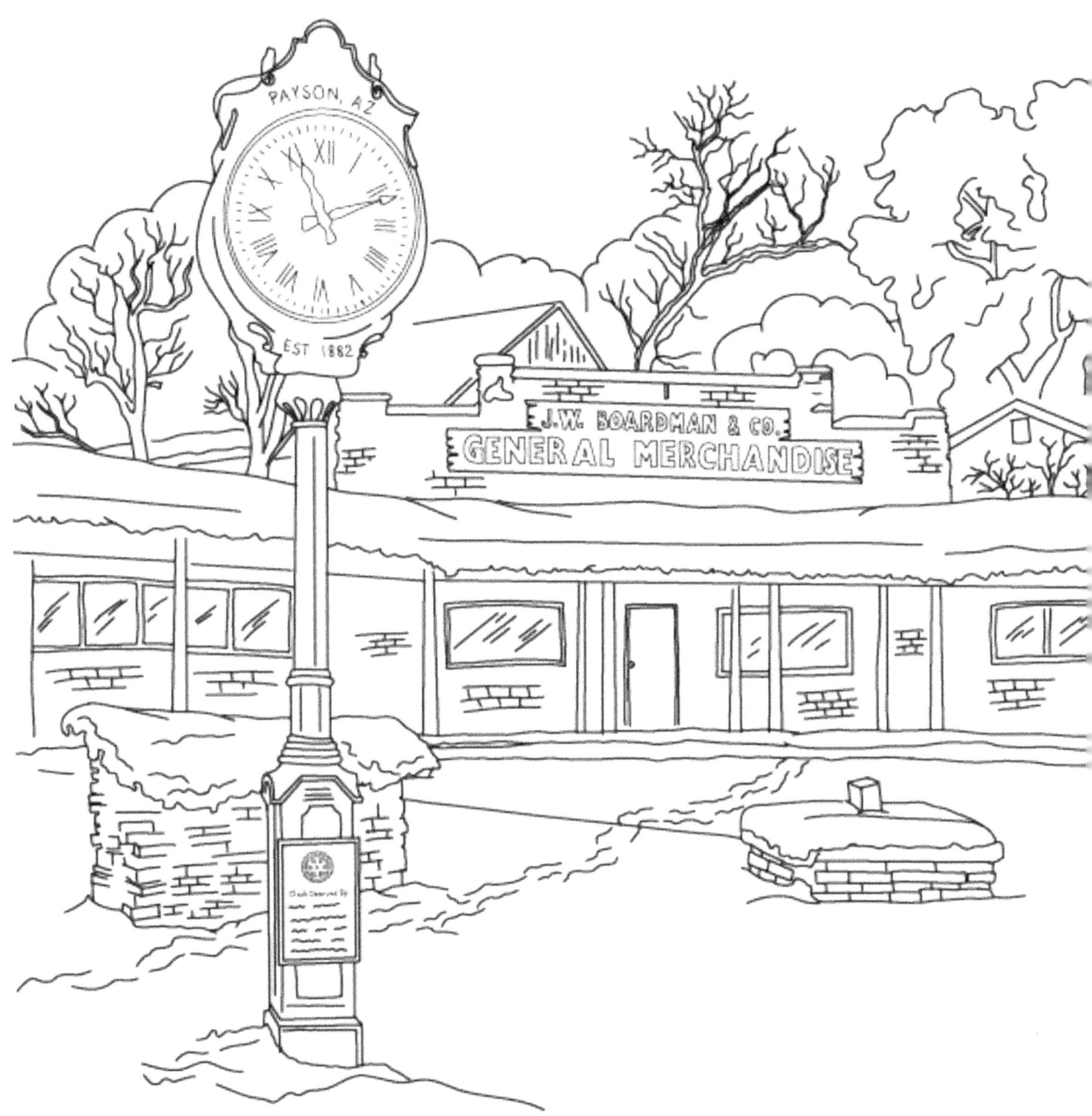

PAYSON, AZ
EST 1882
J.W. BOARDMAN & CO.
GENERAL MERCHANDISE

Zane Grey, the famous author of Western novels, found inspiration in Arizona's rugged landscapes. In 1921, he built a cabin retreat near Payson, nestled under the towering Mogollon Rim. This rustic hideaway became Grey's sanctuary, where he penned some of his most beloved stories.

The cabin, constructed of native pine logs and stone, sat in a picturesque meadow surrounded by towering Ponderosa pines. It was here that Grey immersed himself in the Arizona wilderness, drawing inspiration for novels like "Under the Tonto Rim" and "Code of the West."

Grey's original cabin burned down in the 1990 Dude Fire, but a faithful replica now stands in Green Valley Park in Payson. This reconstruction serves as a museum, allowing visitors to step back in time and experience the environment that fueled Grey's creative spirit.

Fun fact:

Zane Grey was not just a writer, but also an avid outdoorsman. He held several deep sea fishing records and was known to disappear into the Arizona wilderness for weeks at a time, living off the land and gathering material for his stories.

Grey's vivid descriptions of Arizona's landscapes in his novels played a significant role in romanticizing the American West and drawing settlers and tourists to the region. His legacy continues to influence how people perceive and appreciate Arizona's natural beauty.

The Zane Grey Cabin and its history offer a unique blend of literary heritage and Arizona's pioneering spirit, making it a fascinating subject for both history buffs and nature lovers alike.

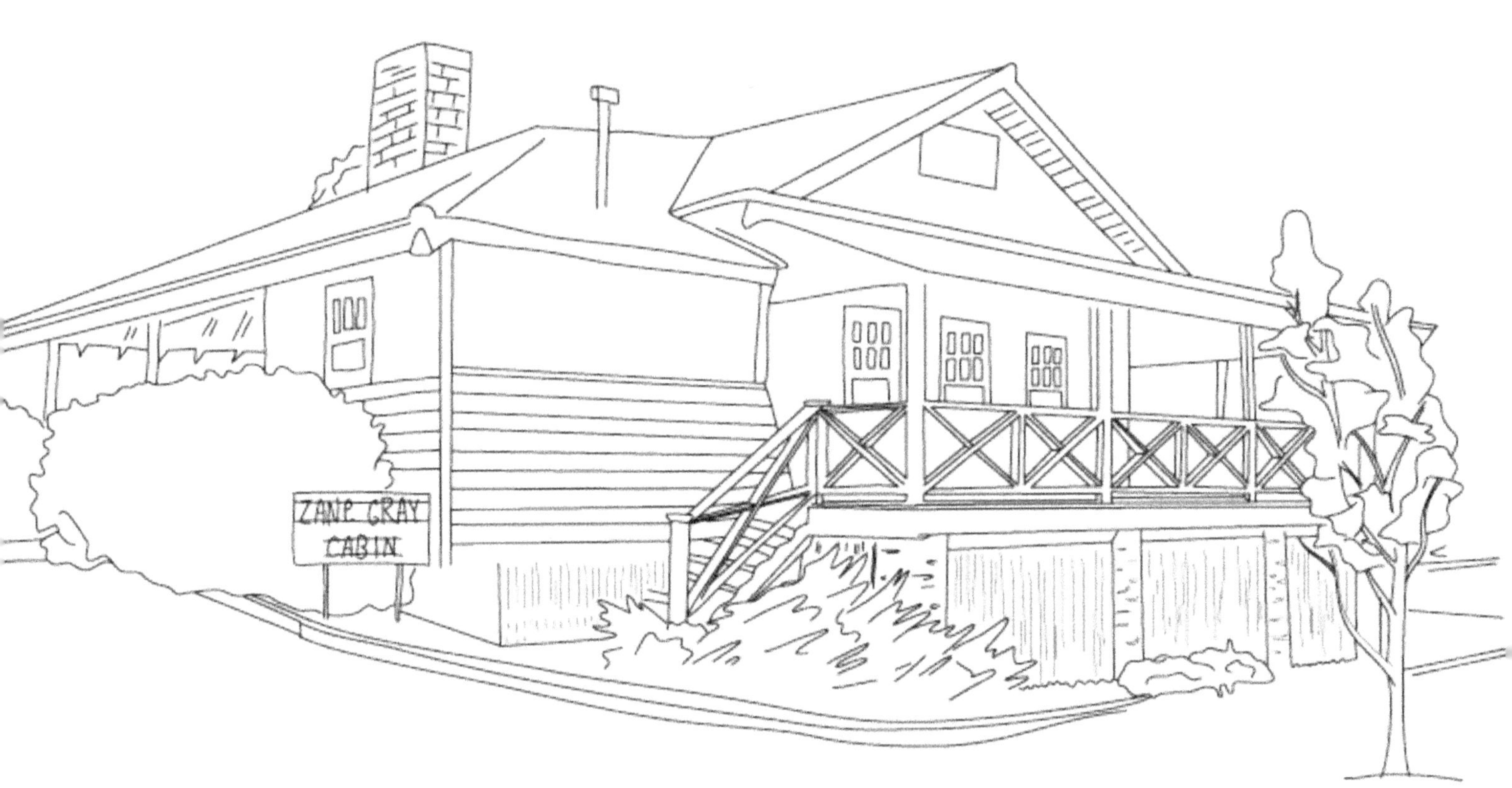

ZANE GRAY
CABIN

Payson Community Garden is a vibrant example of community spirit and sustainable living in the heart of Arizona. Established in February 2012, this garden began as an inspiring interfaith venture, bringing together the Payson First Church of the Nazarene and the Church of Jesus Christ of Latter-Day Saints.

Located on land donated by the Nazarene Church, with construction supervised by the LDS Church, the garden offers individual plots where community members can grow organic produce for personal use and to support local food banks.

This green oasis in Payson serves multiple purposes:

1. It provides fresh, locally-grown produce to community members and food banks.

2. It offers free educational classes each spring on gardening techniques specific to the Payson area.

3. It creates a safe, chemical-free environment for gardeners to meet, share ideas, and help the community.

4. It promotes organic gardening methods, using no pesticides – just natural techniques for pest and weed control.

Fun fact:

The Payson Community Garden showcases how different faith communities can come together to create something beautiful and beneficial for all. This collaborative spirit reflects the broader ethos of many small Arizona towns, where community cooperation often leads to remarkable achievements.

Whether you're an experienced gardener or just starting out, the Payson Community Garden offers a chance to get your hands dirty, learn new skills, and contribute to the community's well-being. It's a living testament to Payson's commitment to sustainability, education, and community service.

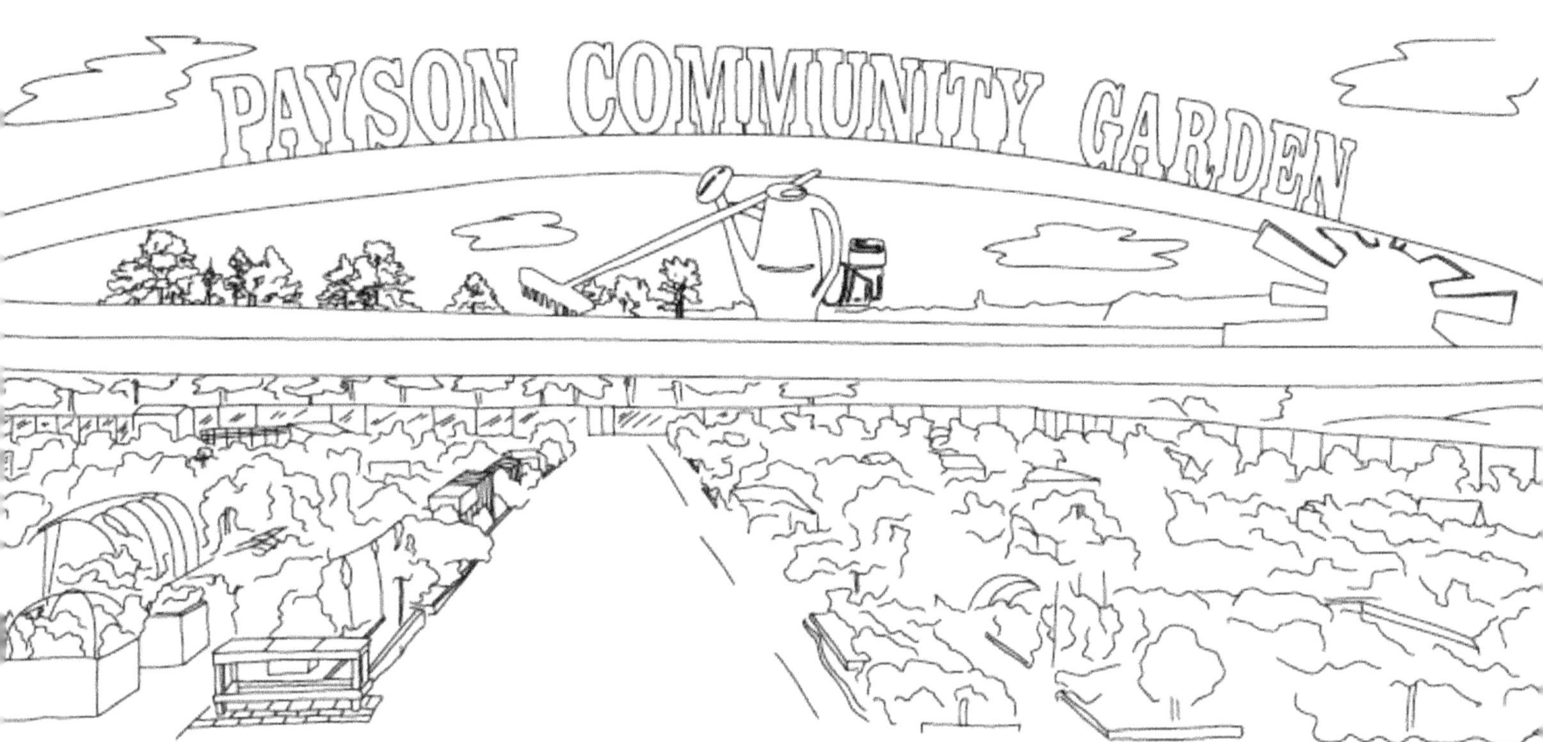
PAYSON COMMUNITY GARDEN

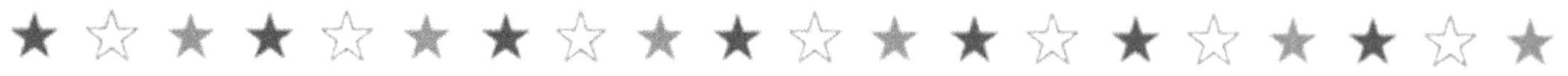

The Ox Bow Inn and Saloon stands as a cherished piece of Payson's history, embodying the rustic charm of Arizona's frontier days. This historic hotel, originally built as the Payson Hotel, has been a landmark in the town since its early days.

William and Estlee Wade, the original owners, constructed this log inn next to their restaurant, the Busy Bee. Interestingly, the design was inspired by the famous Old Faithful Inn in Yellowstone National Park, where William Wade had spent time. This influence is evident in the rustic, grand lodge-style architecture that gives the Ox Bow its unique character.

In 1945, the business entered a new chapter when Jimmy Cox took over and expanded the property. It was Cox who renamed it the Ox Bow Inn, the name by which it's still known today.

Fun fact:

The Ox Bow Inn's design, inspired by the Old Faithful Inn, brings a touch of America's first national park to the heart of Arizona. This architectural connection creates a unique blend of Western frontier styles, bridging the gap between the Rocky Mountains and Arizona's high country.

Over the years, the Ox Bow Inn and Saloon has become more than just a place to play - it's a living museum of Payson's history. Its log construction and period details offer visitors a glimpse into Arizona's past, while its continued operation keeps that history alive and accessible.

Today, the Ox Bow remains a popular destination for both tourists and locals, offering a taste of old Arizona charm in the midst of modern Payson. It stands as a testament to the town's rich history and enduring spirit.

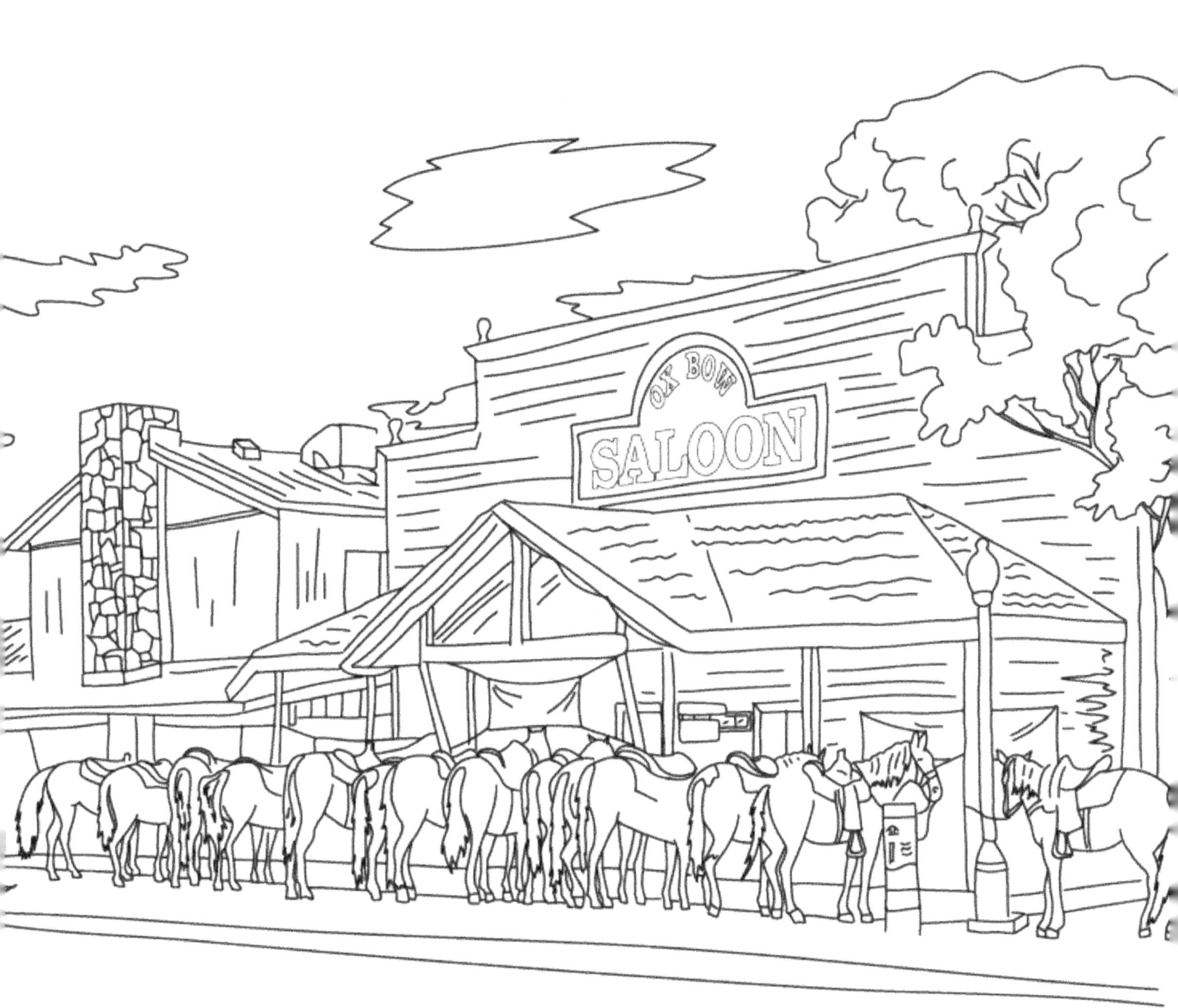
OX BOW
SALOON

Creekside Tavern: A Hub of Local Flavor and Relaxation

Creekside Tavern is a beloved local establishment in Christopher Creek, offering a welcoming atmosphere and hearty meals for visitors and residents alike. Known for its rustic charm and friendly service, the tavern is a perfect spot to unwind after a day of outdoor activities.

Creekside Tavern serves a variety of comfort foods, including burgers, steaks, and fresh fish, making it a popular choice for those looking to enjoy a satisfying meal in a cozy setting.

Often hosting live music and community events, Creekside Tavern is not just a place to eat but a social hub where locals and visitors can connect and enjoy entertainment.

With its wood-paneled interior and rustic decor, the tavern exudes the charm of a traditional mountain lodge. The relaxed environment and scenic views of Christopher Creek from the outdoor seating area enhance the dining experience, making it a memorable stop for all who visit.

Unique Local Lore: The Mogollon Monster

Christopher Creek has been featured in popular media, including an episode of Animal Planet's "Finding Bigfoot," due to local legends of the "Mogollon Monster," Arizona's version of Bigfoot. This adds a touch of mystery and intrigue to the area, enhancing its appeal to adventurous visitors.

Outdoor Activities and Attractions

Christopher Creek is a haven for outdoor enthusiasts, offering numerous activities such as hiking, fishing, and horseback riding.

Notable spots include:

Highline Trail: Offering breathtaking views of the Mogollon Rim, this trail is a favorite for hikers and mountain bikers.

Fishing Spots: Christopher Creek and nearby Tonto Creek are regularly stocked with rainbow trout, making them ideal for fishing.

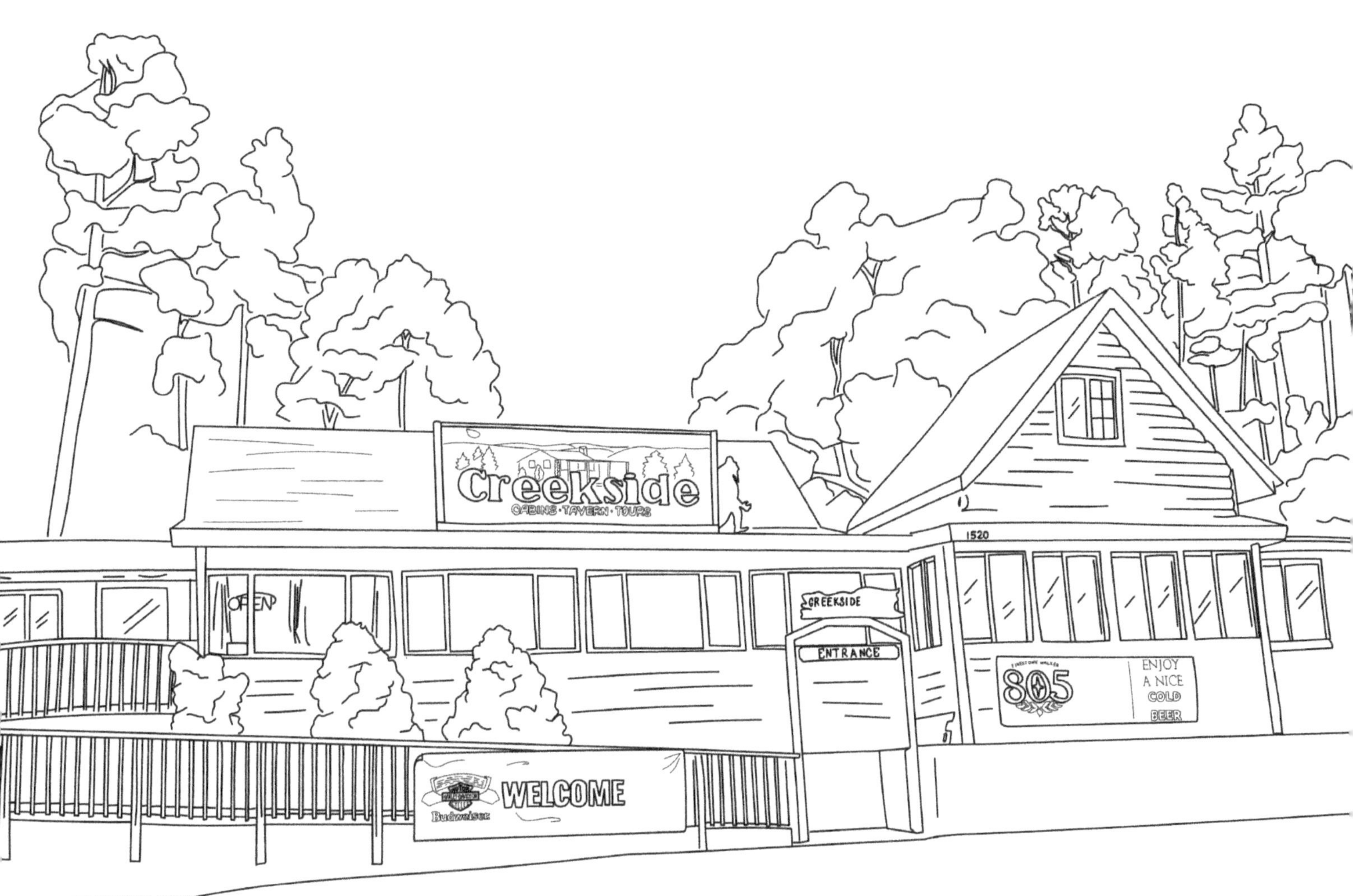

Creekside
CABINS · TAVERN · TOURS
OPEN
1520
CREEKSIDE
ENTRANCE
805
ENJOY
A NICE
COLD
BEER
Budweiser
WELCOME

Tall Pines Market: Your One-Stop Shop in Christopher Creek

Tall Pines Market is the go-to place for groceries, supplies, and local goods in Christopher Creek. Conveniently located and well-stocked, it serves the needs of both residents and visitors, ensuring they have everything required for a comfortable stay.

The market offers a wide range of products, including fresh produce, dairy, meats, and pantry staples. Whether you're stocking up for a cabin stay or just passing through, Tall Pines Market has you covered.

Emphasizing local artisans and producers, the market features a variety of local goods, from handmade crafts to regional specialties, providing a taste of the area's culture and craftsmanship.

Given the popularity of outdoor activities in the area, the market also stocks essential camping and hiking gear, making it easy for adventurers to prepare for their trips.

Tall Pines Market serves as a community hub where locals catch up and visitors can get insider tips on the best spots to explore around Christopher Creek. The friendly staff are always ready to help, providing a warm welcome to all who enter.

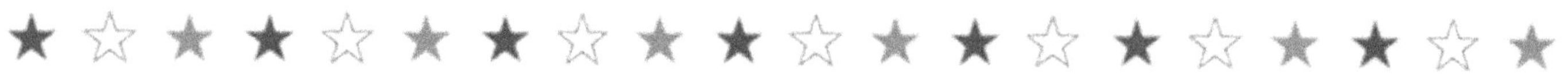

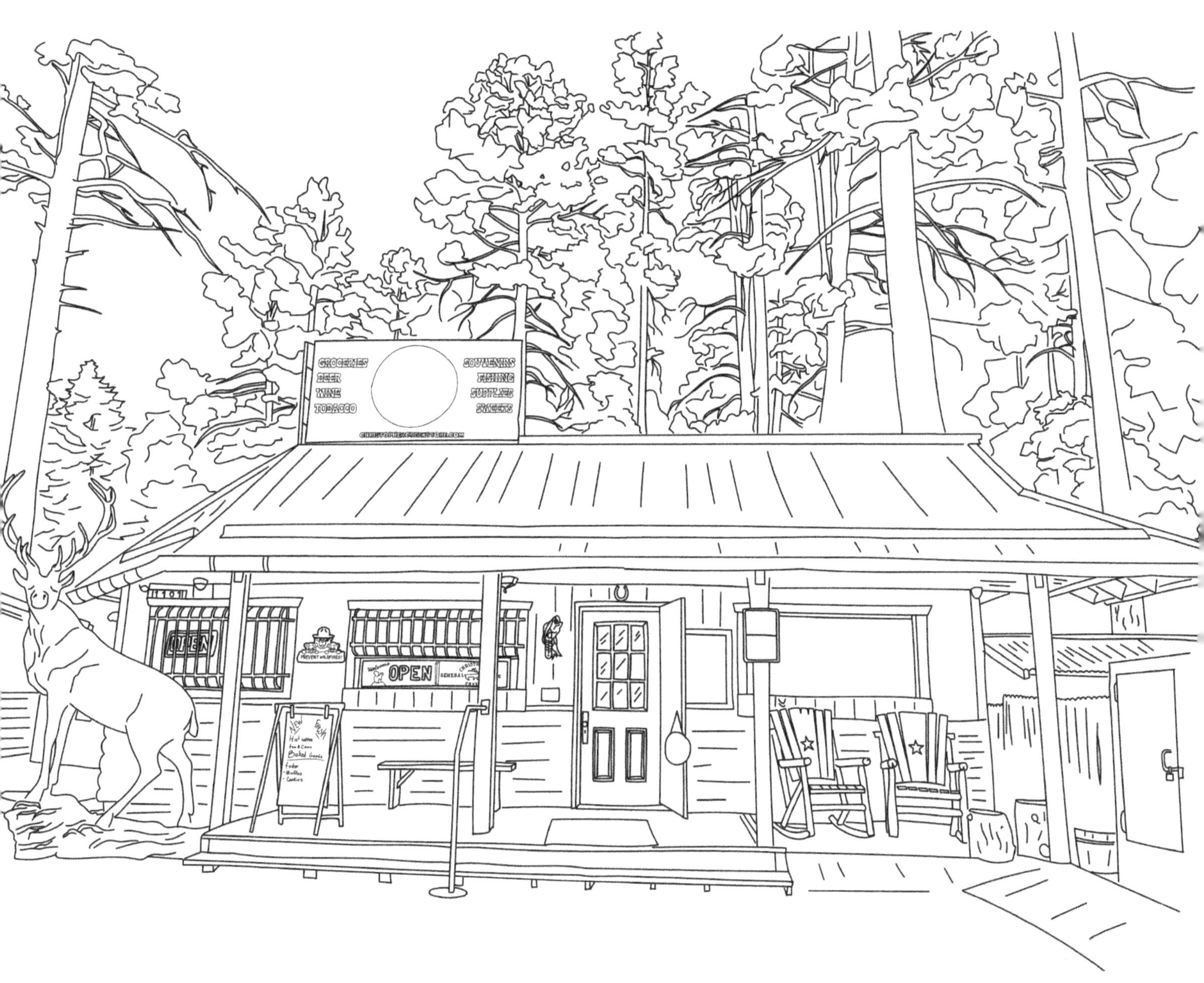

GROCERIES
BEER
WINE
TOBACCO
SOUVENIRS
FISHING
SUPPLIES
SWEETS
CHRISTOPHERKENNEDYSTOHL.COM
PREVENT WILDFIRES!
OPEN
OPEN
NEW
FRESH
Hot coffee
Tea & Cocoa
Baked Goods
- Fudge
- Muffins
- Cookies

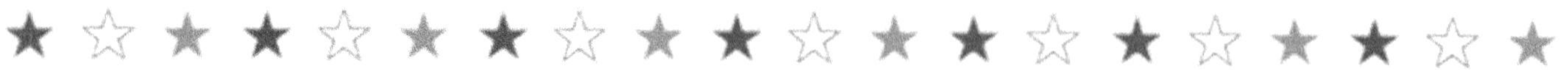

Tonto Creek Fish Hatchery: Sustaining Arizona's Aquatic Life

Located in the heart of the Tonto National Forest, the Tonto Creek Fish Hatchery is a cornerstone of Arizona's efforts to maintain healthy fish populations in its lakes and rivers. This hatchery, established in 1937, is dedicated to breeding and stocking various species of fish, playing a vital role in the conservation of aquatic life and supporting recreational fishing across the state.

The hatchery utilizes a series of raceways, ponds, and tanks to rear fish from eggs to mature adults. The process begins with the careful collection of eggs, which are then fertilized and incubated under optimal conditions. Once the eggs hatch, the fry are nurtured and monitored until they are ready for release.

Historical Significance: The Tonto Creek Fish Hatchery was constructed during the Great Depression as part of a federal effort to create jobs and support local economies. It has since become a key institution in Arizona's wildlife conservation landscape.

Sustainable Practices: The hatchery employs sustainable practices to minimize its environmental impact. This includes water recirculation systems and efforts to reduce waste.

Recreational Impact: By stocking fish in Arizona's lakes and rivers, the hatchery supports recreational fishing, which is a popular pastime and an important economic driver in the state.

Fun Fact:

The Apache trout, which is a major focus of the Tonto Creek Fish Hatchery, was once on the brink of extinction. Thanks to concerted conservation efforts, including those at this hatchery, the species has made a remarkable recovery and serves as a symbol of successful wildlife management.

Visitors to the Tonto Creek Fish Hatchery can enjoy a self-guided tour of the facilities, where they can observe the fish rearing process and learn about the hatchery's conservation efforts. The surrounding Tonto National Forest offers ample opportunities for hiking, birdwatching, and enjoying the natural beauty of Arizona.

The Tonto Creek Fish Hatchery is not only a hub for fish production but also a testament to Arizona's commitment to preserving its natural resources. It provides an essential service to the state's aquatic ecosystems while offering educational and recreational opportunities for the public.

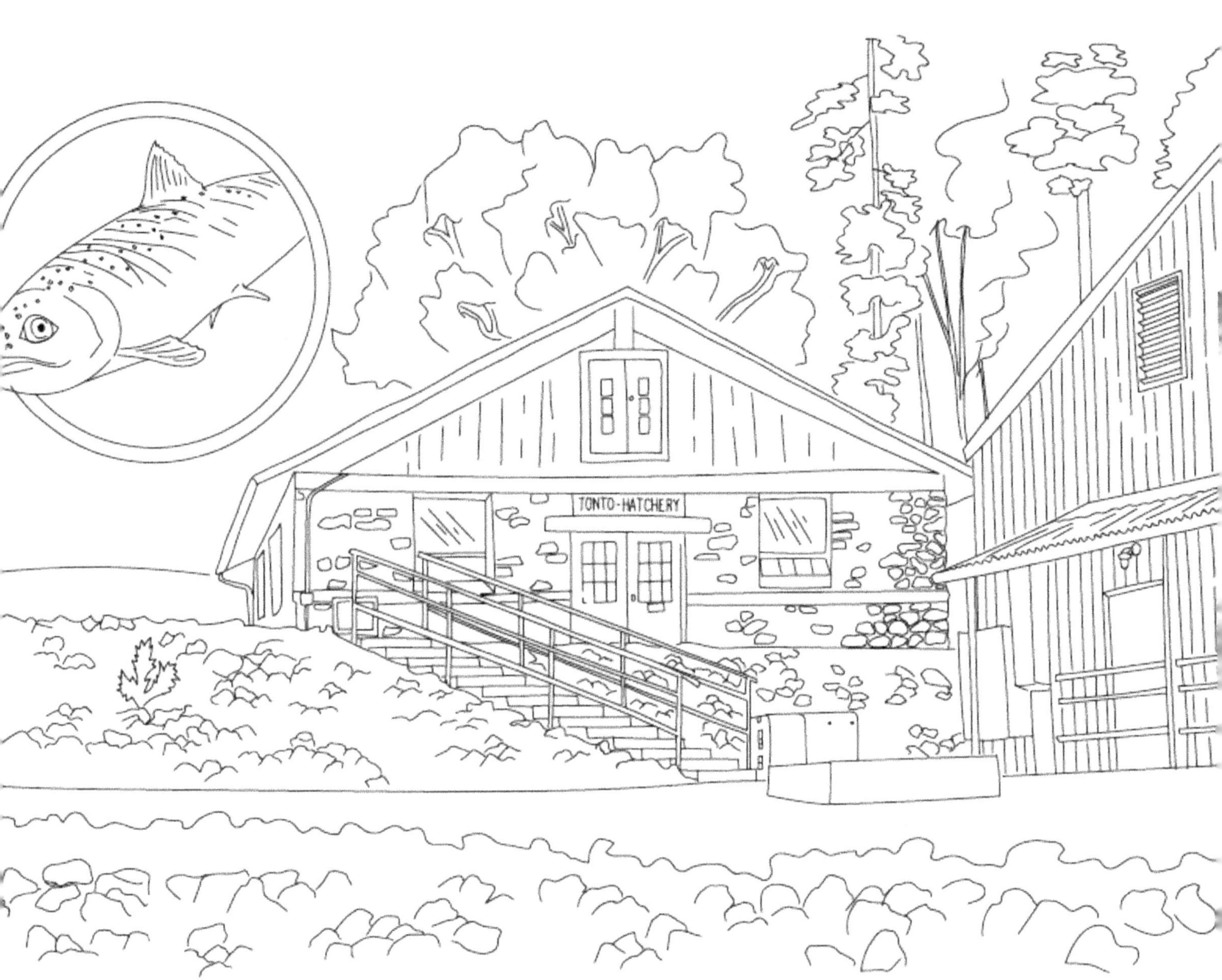
TONTO-HATCHERY

Diamond Point: A Crystal Hunting Adventure

Diamond Point is a popular rockhounding site located about 40 minutes from Payson, Arizona. Known for its quartz crystals, often referred to as "Payson Diamonds," it attracts both amateur and experienced collectors.

Surface Collecting: The site is open year-round for surface collecting of quartz crystals. Digging is limited to protect the environment and is only allowed from October through February. Collectors are permitted to use small hand tools like trowels and gardening picks. The area offers beautiful forested landscapes and is part of the Tonto National Forest. The collection site spans about 35 acres and includes dry washes and riverbeds where crystals are often found.

Best Times to Visit: Late spring or early summer after the snow melts is ideal for surface hunting. However, if you prefer digging, plan your visit in early October to avoid winter weather. Finding significant crystals can take time. Surface hunting can be fruitful, especially after rains that wash away dirt, revealing hidden crystals

Visiting Diamond Point offers not just the thrill of finding beautiful quartz crystals but also an opportunity to enjoy the stunning natural surroundings and perhaps a brush with local legends. Make sure to respect the environment and enjoy your time exploring this unique Arizona treasure.

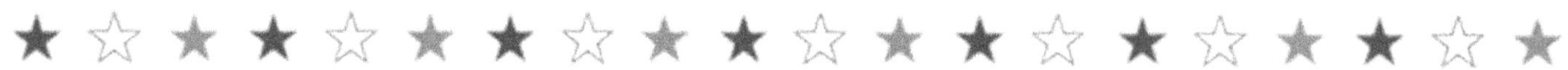

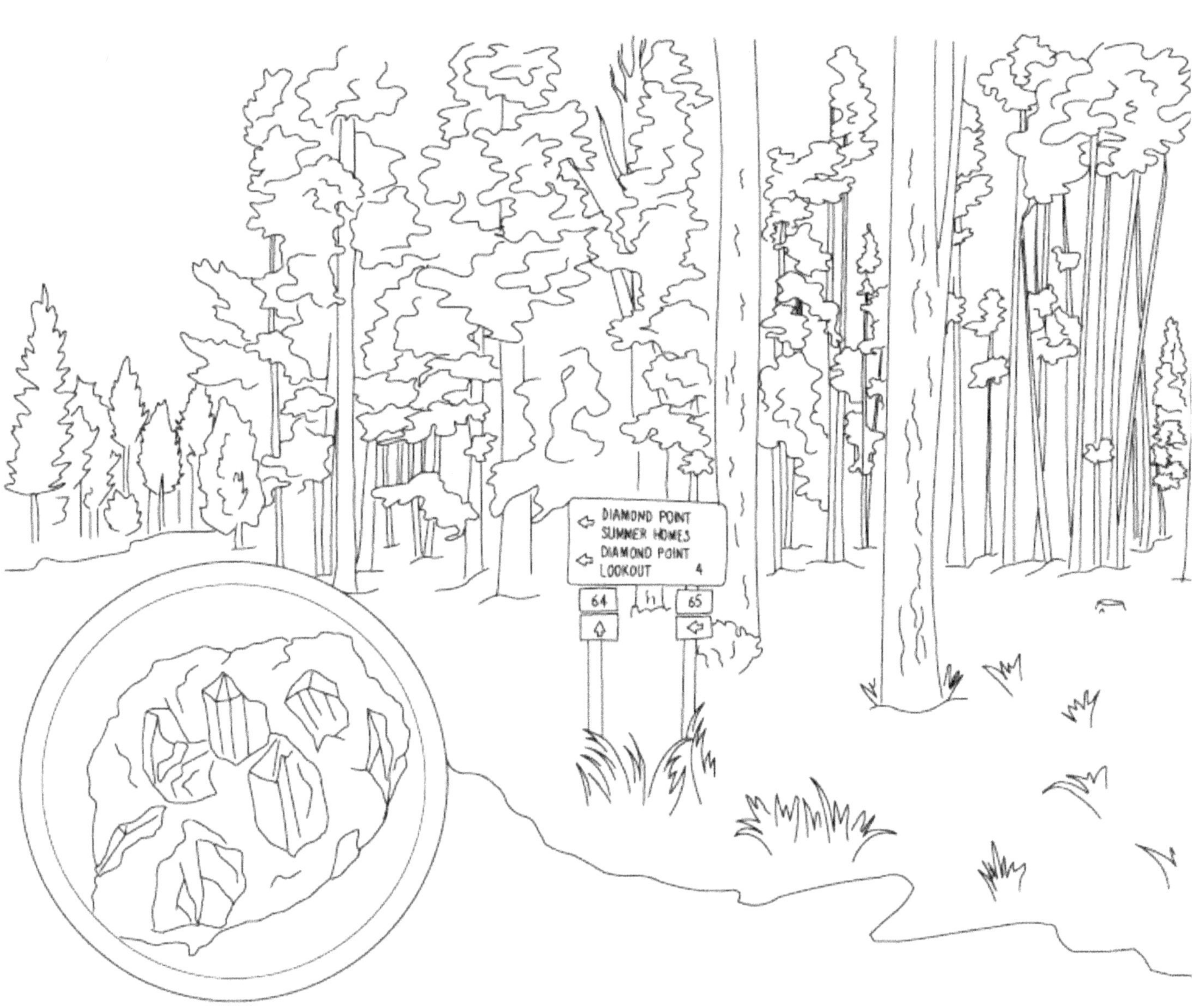

DIAMOND POINT
SUMMER HOMES
DIAMOND POINT
LOOKOUT   4
64
65

Kohl's Ranch Lodge: A Tranquil Retreat
in the Heart of Nature

Kohl's Ranch Lodge, Located at the base of the Mogollon Rim, the lodge is surrounded by stunning natural landscapes and is a serene retreat nestled at the base of the Mogollon Rim, shaded by the vast expanse of the largest Ponderosa Pine Forest in the world. This picturesque lodge offers a perfect escape from the hustle and bustle of daily life, providing guests with a relaxing and nature-filled experience.

The lodge offers a range of recreational activities to suit all interests: Swimming Pool Guests can relax poolside, soaking in the fresh mountain air, for those who wish to stay active during their stay, there is an Arcade and Mini-Golf Course.

Horseback Riding and Fishing, Explore the scenic surroundings or enjoy fishing in nearby streams.

Kohl's Ranch Lodge exudes a friendly and casual atmosphere, making it a welcoming destination for families, couples, and solo travelers. The cozy interiors and rustic decor enhance the mountain lodge feel, ensuring guests feel right at home amidst the beautiful natural setting.

Whether you're seeking relaxation or adventure, Kohl's Ranch Lodge provides a perfect blend of both, with comfortable accommodations and a wide array of activities to enjoy during your stay.

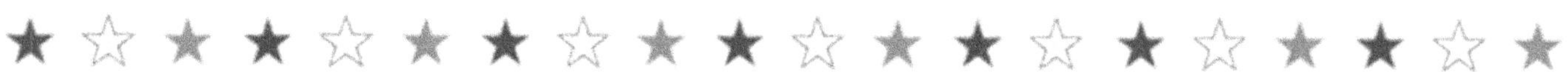

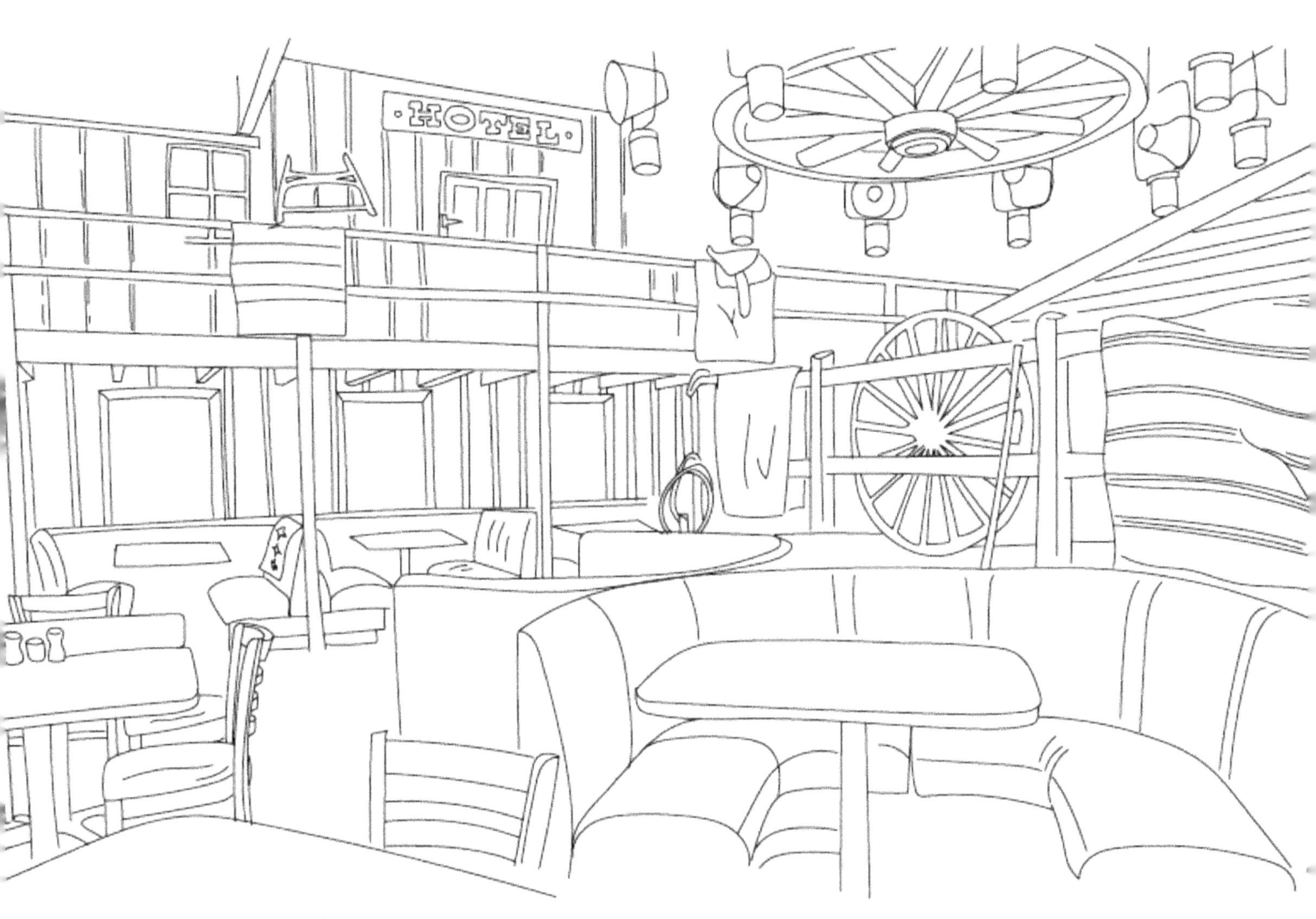
·HOTEL·

Golfing in Payson

Nestled in the majestic Mogollon Rim country of Arizona, amidst the world's largest stand of Ponderosa Pines, lie two remarkable golf communities: Chaparral Pines and The Rim Golf Club. These exclusive enclaves offer a unique blend of natural beauty, world-class golf, and luxurious mountain living, just a scenic 75-90 minute drive from Scottsdale.

The Ponderosa Pines that dominate the landscape are a sight to behold. These towering giants can reach heights of 100-150 feet, their distinctive puzzle-bark trunks and spreading canopies creating a verdant oasis in the high country. The forests here provide habitat for diverse wildlife, including bald and golden eagles, ospreys, and great blue herons.

Both communities boast championship golf courses that harmonize with the natural terrain. Chaparral Pines' course, designed by David Graham and Gary Panks, and The Rim's course, crafted by Tom Weiskopf and Jay Morrish, offer challenging play amidst breathtaking scenery. Golfers might find themselves pausing mid-swing to admire the panoramic vistas of the Mogollon Rim.

Fun fact:

The area enjoys a four-season climate, with summer temperatures about 20 degrees cooler than Phoenix. Winter brings crisp, sunny days and star-filled nights, while fall paints the landscape in a palette of autumn colors.

Beyond golf, these communities offer a wealth of amenities. Chaparral Pines' 27,000-square-foot clubhouse, with its rough-hewn timber beams and crackling fireplaces, serves as a welcoming gathering place. The Trailhead Park provides fitness facilities, swimming pools, and sports courts for active lifestyles.

Whether you're teeing off on a world-class golf course, hiking through pine-scented forests, or simply relaxing on your deck watching the sunset paint the Rim, these communities offer a slice of high-country paradise. They represent the perfect blend of natural beauty and refined living, a testament to Arizona's diverse landscapes and lifestyles.

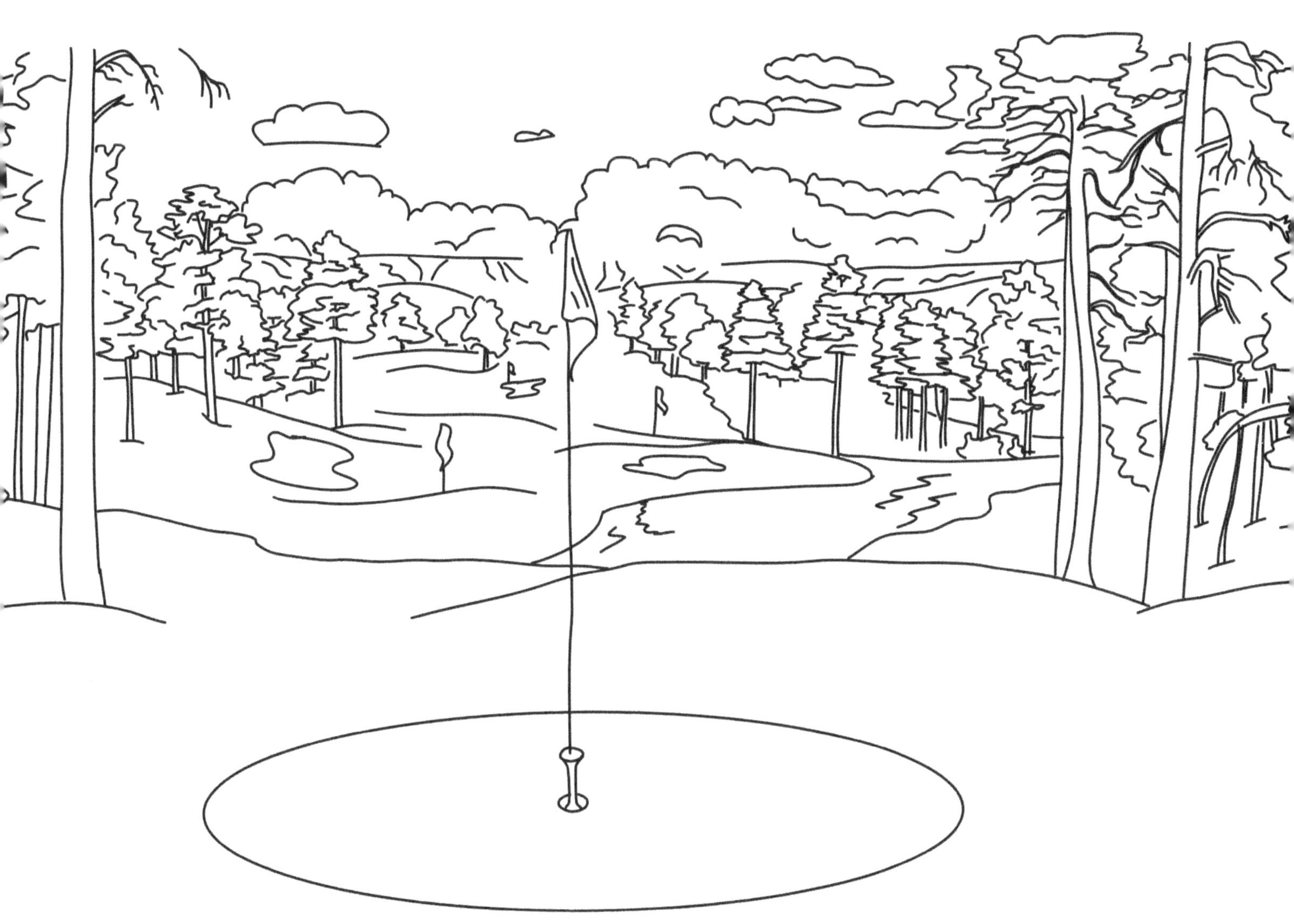

Pine Creek Canyon Lavender Farm: A Fragrant Escape in Arizona

Shaded by the towering treetops of the largest Ponderosa Pine Forest in the world, Pine Creek Canyon Lavender Farm rests peacefully in the charming mountain town of Pine, Arizona. This family-owned farm is a haven of tranquility and natural beauty, offering visitors a unique experience surrounded by over 5,000 lavender plants.

The farm's history dates back to the early 1900s when Almay Moroni and Rosetta Hunt settled in Pine and began farming. The original log cabin, now used for lavender drying, was built in 1890 as storage for the Hunt family. The current owners, Terry and Rick Vesci, have preserved this historical charm while cultivating the land with lavender.

Pine Creek Canyon Lavender Farm utilizes natural spring water from Pine Creek for irrigation. This pristine water source nourishes the lavender plants, enhancing their quality and aromatic properties. The high elevation and dry air of the region contribute to the production of highly concentrated oils within the lavender, making it exceptionally fragrant and beneficial.

Fun Facts

Elk-Resistant Crops -The decision to grow lavender was influenced by the fact that elk, which are common in the area, do not eat lavender. This practical choice has resulted in a flourishing lavender farm.

Culinary Delights: The farm's culinary classes teach visitors how to use lavender in various recipes, from sweet to savory dishes. Royal Velvet and Provence varieties are especially popular in cooking.

The farm grows three main types of lavender:

Royal Velvet: Known for its sweet flavor, ideal for baking and confectionery.

Provence: Used in savory dishes, similar to rosemary.

Grosso: Highly aromatic, perfect for essential oils, sachets, and bouquets.

Annual Lavender Festival: The farm hosts a yearly Lavender Festival that celebrates the lavender harvest with workshops, events, and a variety of lavender products. This festival is a major attraction for both locals and tourists.

Pine Creek Canyon Lavender Farm stands as a testament to sustainable farming and historical preservation, offering visitors a unique blend of natural beauty, aromatic lavender, and rich history.

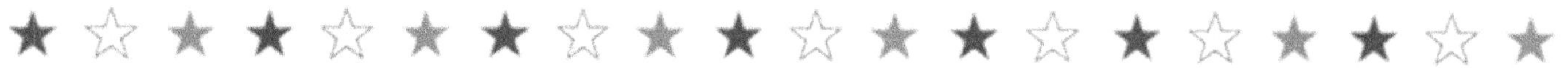

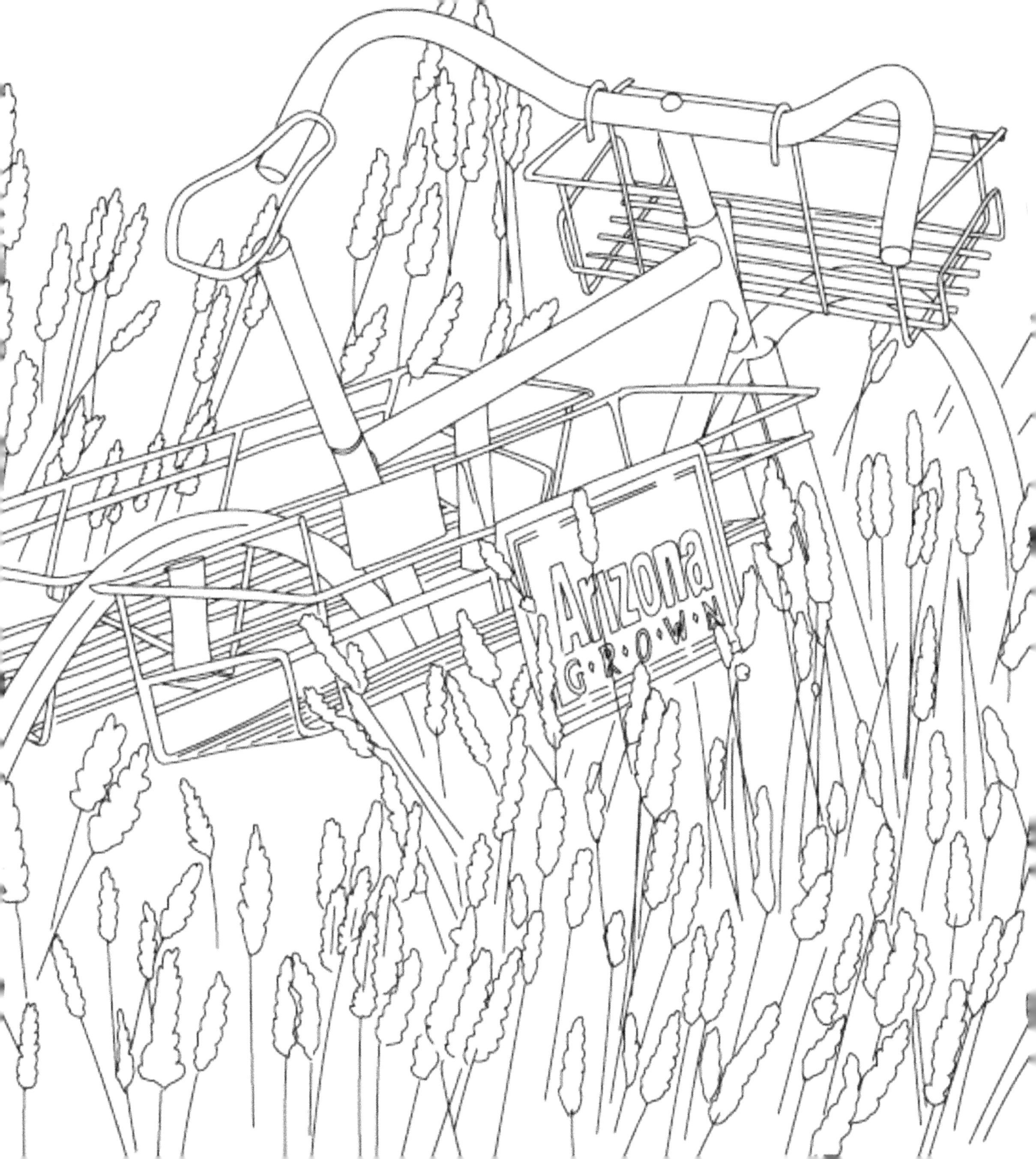

Arizona
G·R·O·W·N

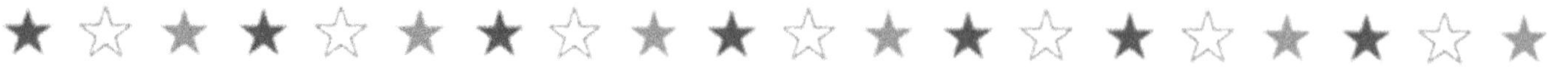

The Honey Stand: A Sweet Stop in Pine, Arizona

Shaded by the towering treetops of the largest Ponderosa Pine Forest in the world, The Honey Stand in Pine, Arizona offers a delightful array of local honey and other natural products. Situated in one of the oldest buildings in Pine, this charming roadside market has been a favorite stop for travelers and locals alike since it opened in 1980.

A Variety of Honey

The Honey Stand boasts a collection of pure, raw Arizona honey, each with its own unique flavor profile. Some of the popular varieties include:

- **Orange Blossom Honey**: Known for its light, citrusy flavor.
- **Mesquite Honey**: Offers a rich, robust taste.
- **Wild Mountain Pecan Honey**: A distinctive, nutty flavor.
- **Desert Clover Honey**: Mild and floral.
- **Cat Claw Honey**: Unique and slightly spicy.
- **Pine Wildflower Honey**: A blend of local wildflower nectars.

Fun Facts

Bee's Journey: It takes a bee 10,000,000 trips to collect enough nectar to make one pound of honey. Thankfully, visitors only need to make one stop at The Honey Stand to enjoy the fruits of this labor.

Historic Building: The Honey Stand operates out of one of the oldest buildings in Pine, adding a touch of historical charm to the shopping experience.

Whether you're a local or just passing through, The Honey Stand offers a sweet and memorable experience with its wide array of natural products and welcoming atmosphere.

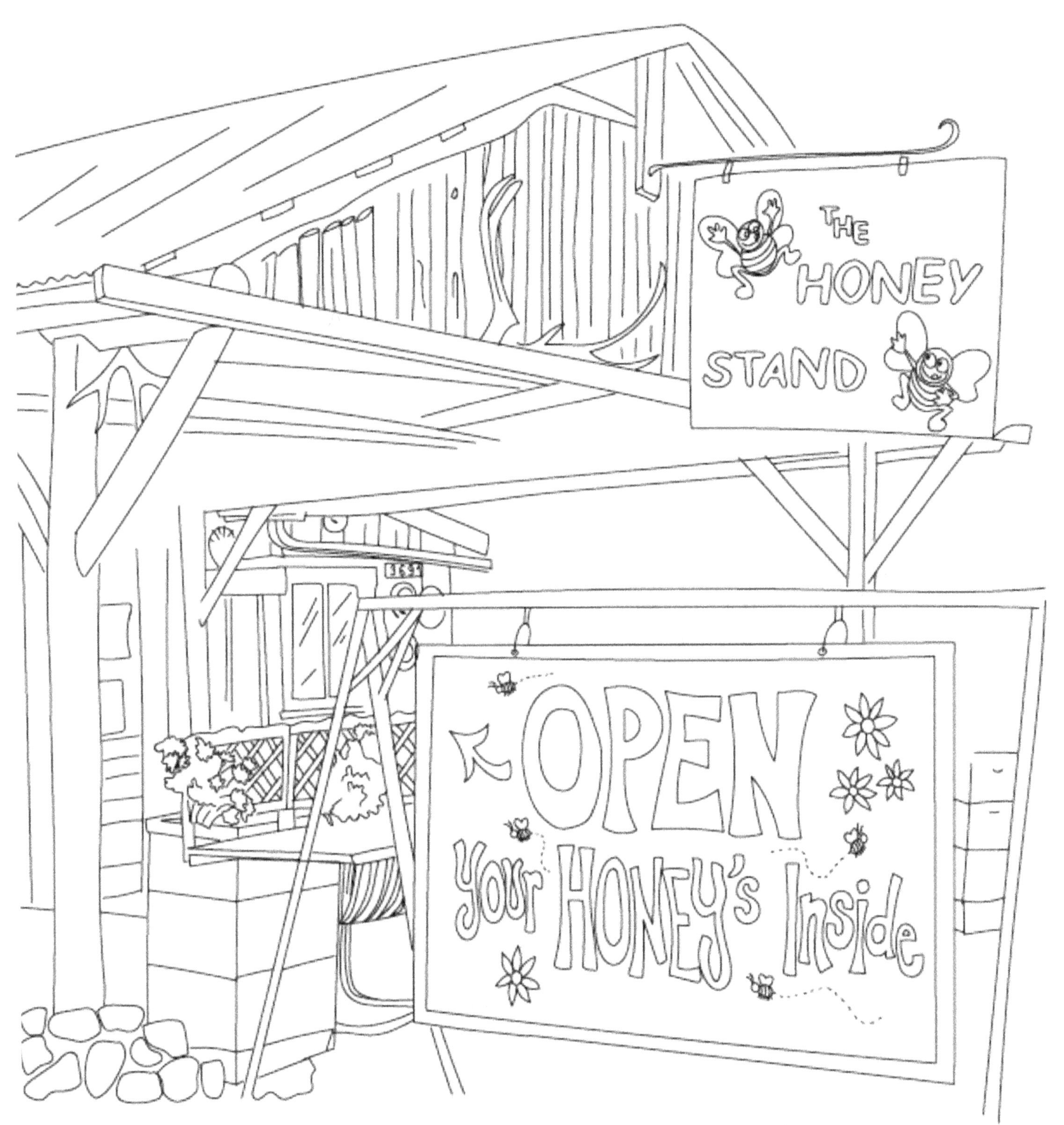

THE
HONEY
STAND
OPEN
Your HONEY's Inside

Rocky the Elk: Payson's Iconic Roundabout Sculpture

Rocky the Elk is a prominent bronze statue located in a roundabout at the northern entrance of Payson, Arizona. This majestic sculpture is part of the Payson Gateway Project, aimed at beautifying the town and highlighting its connection to local wildlife and nature.

The bronze elk statue was created to celebrate the natural beauty and wildlife of the Payson area, which is known for its significant elk population. The statue not only serves as a stunning piece of art but also as a symbol of Payson's commitment to preserving its natural surroundings and promoting wildlife conservation.

The installation of Rocky the Elk was made possible through the efforts of the Friends of Payson Parks and Recreation and the broader community. A fundraiser was organized to cover the costs of the statue, with over 95% of the financial goal met through donations. The community's support highlights the local pride and dedication to enhancing the town's aesthetic appeal and environmental awareness.

Rocky the Elk is prominently placed at the northern roundabout entrance to Payson, making it one of the first sights to greet visitors entering the town. This strategic location not only enhances the visual appeal of the gateway but also underscores the importance of wildlife in the region's identity.

The statue of Rocky the Elk stands as a testament to Payson's rich natural heritage and the community's efforts to celebrate and preserve it. Visitors and locals alike can appreciate the artistry and symbolism of this impressive sculpture as they explore the beautiful town of Payson.

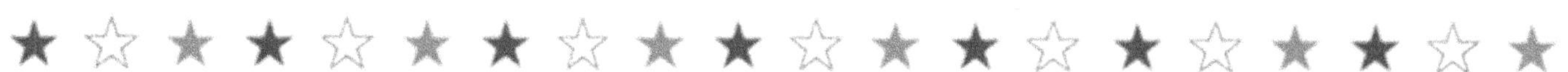

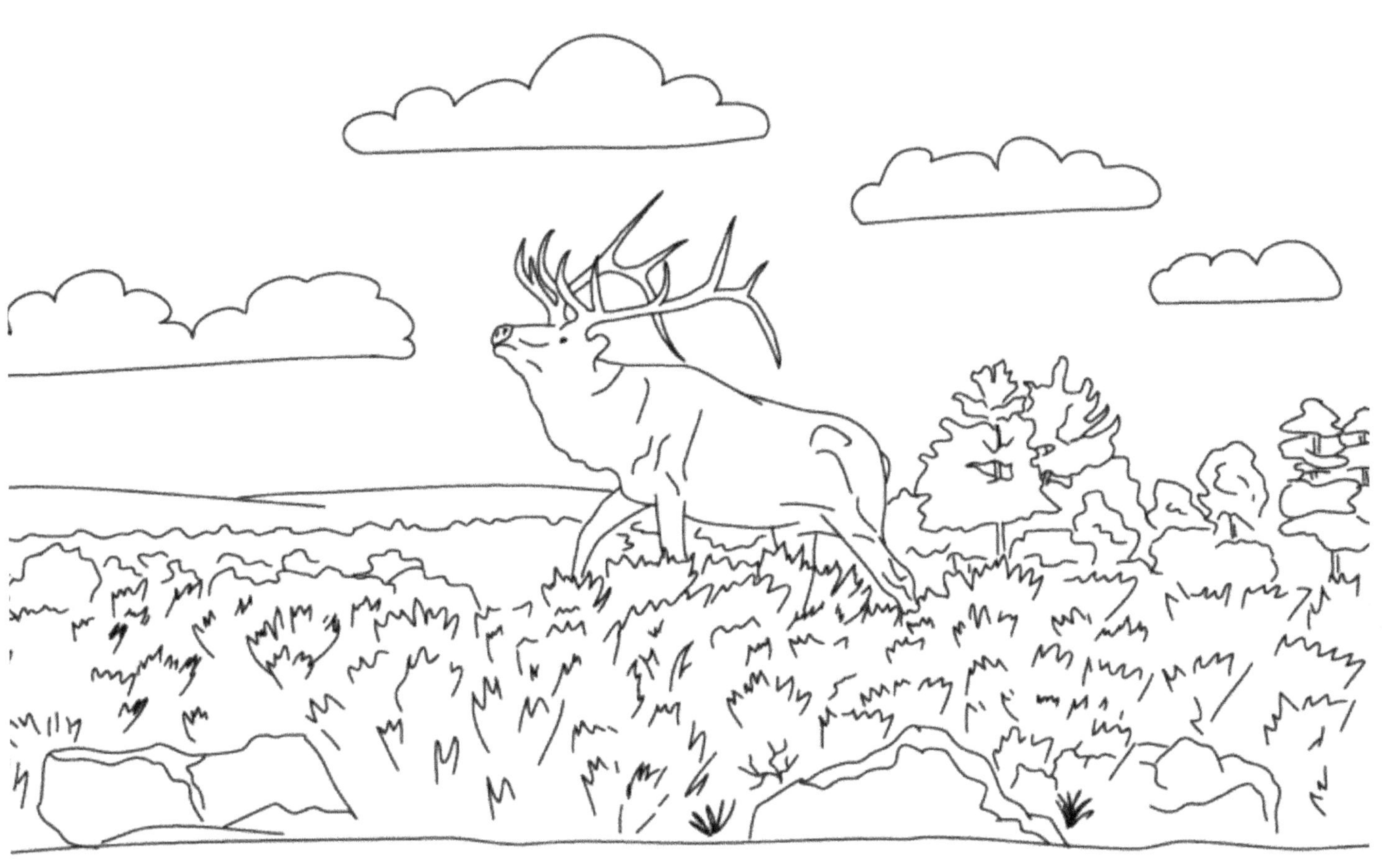

Water Wheel Falls Hike: A Natural Oasis in Arizona

Shaded by the towering treetops of the Tonto National Forest, the Water Wheel Falls Hike near Payson, Arizona, offers an enchanting outdoor experience. This scenic trail, following the East Verde River, is known for its stunning waterfalls, crystal-clear pools, and lush greenery, making it a must-visit for nature lovers.

Trail Overview

Length 1.6 miles round trip
Difficulty: Moderate
Elevation Gain: 150 feet
Best Time to Visit: April through September

The hike begins at the Water Wheel Day Use Area and meanders alongside the East Verde River. As you walk, you are greeted by the melodic sound of rushing water and the sight of vibrant foliage and towering cliffs.

Waterfalls and Pools: The trail features multiple waterfalls, including the main Water Wheel Falls, which cascades into an inviting emerald swimming hole surrounded by red granite walls.

Fun Facts

The hike is perfect for escaping the Arizona heat, with numerous spots to cool off in the river and pools.

The trail is suitable for dogs on a leash, making it a great outing for furry friends.

Old Water Wheel: At the trailhead, remnants of an old water wheel are visible, giving the trail its name and a touch of historical charm.

Cliff Jumping For the adventurous, there are spots for cliff jumping, but caution is advised to ensure the water depth is sufficient and free of hazards.

The Water Wheel Falls Hike is a beautiful, short adventure offering a great reward with its stunning waterfalls and swimming holes. It's an ideal way to experience the natural beauty of Arizona while enjoying a refreshing dip in the clear waters of the East Verde River.

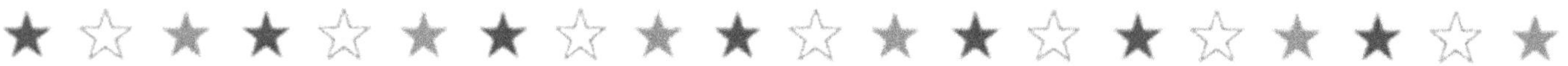

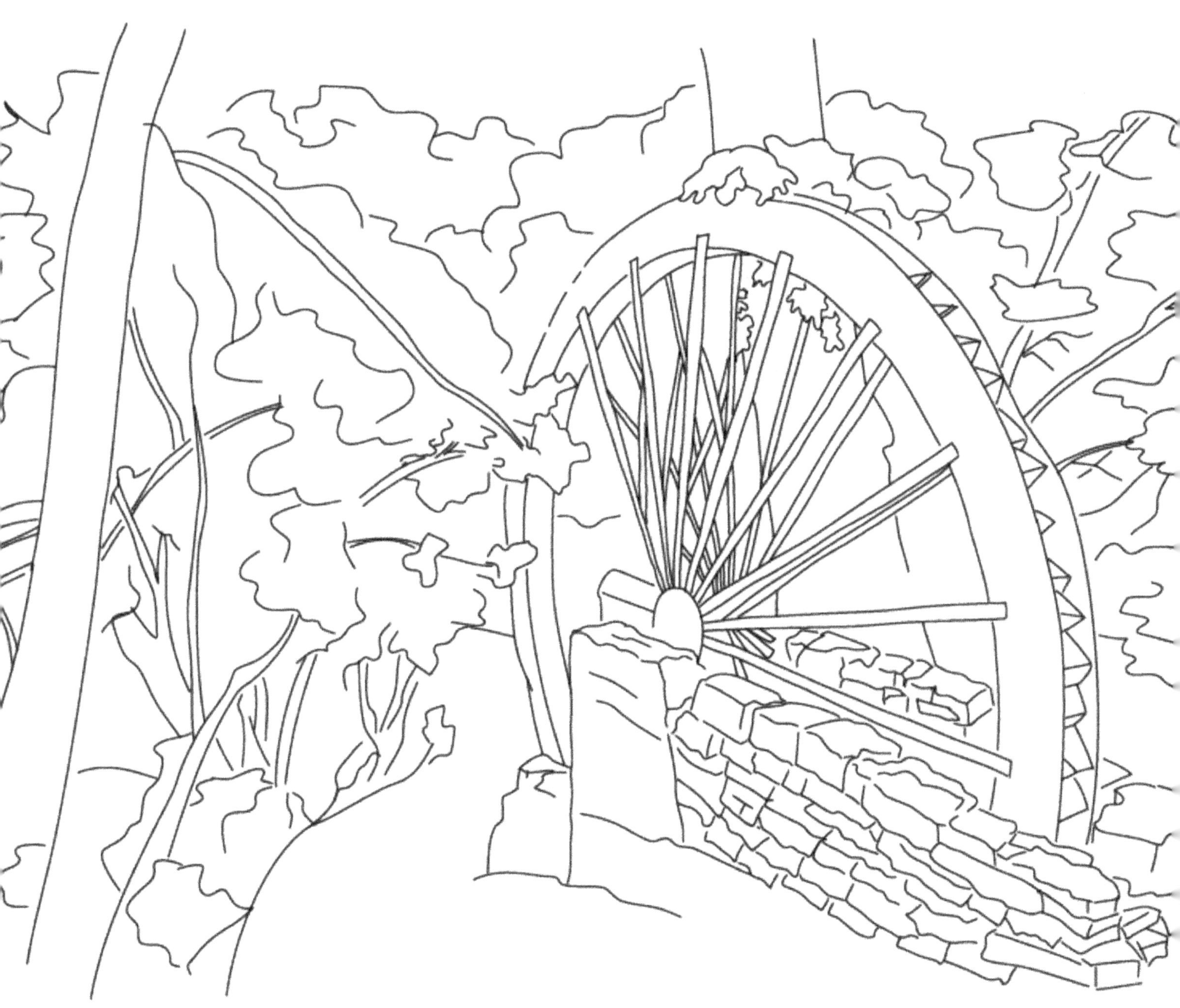

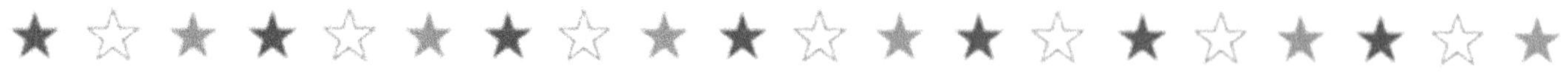

East Verde River Trail: A Scenic Adventure in Arizona

Shaded by the majestic trees of the Tonto National Forest, the East Verde River Trail near Payson, Arizona, offers a delightful outdoor experience. This trail winds through picturesque landscapes, following the East Verde River and providing hikers with stunning views and serene environments.

Trail Overview

Length Approximately 16 miles one-way
Difficulty: Moderate
Elevation Gain: 1,468 feet
Best Time to Visit: Spring through Fall

The trail begins just west of downtown Payson and extends through the Tonto National Forest. It features a variety of terrains, including dirt roads, river crossings, and rocky sections. The hike is suitable for stock SUVs with high clearance and 4WD, making it a popular choice for off-road enthusiasts as well.

Fun Facts

River Crossings: The trail includes several river crossings, with the most notable being at 12.7 miles. These crossings provide a refreshing break and add an element of adventure to the hike.

Highlights

Scenic Views: The trail offers breathtaking views of the East Verde River and its surrounding landscapes. Hikers can enjoy the beauty of the Mazatzal Wilderness and the Mogollon Rim. Wildlife: The area is rich in wildlife, offering opportunities to spot various animals and birds along the trail.

Historical Sites: The trail passes by the ruins of the Cracker Jack Mine, adding a touch of historical interest to the journey.

Camping Opportunities: there are numerous dispersed camping sites along the trail, making it a great option for an extended outdoor adventure.

Off-Roading: The trail is rated as moderate for off-roading, with a few challenging sections that require careful navigation.

The East Verde River Trail offers a perfect blend of scenic beauty, historical intrigue, and outdoor adventure, making it a must-visit for hiking and off-roading enthusiasts in Arizona.

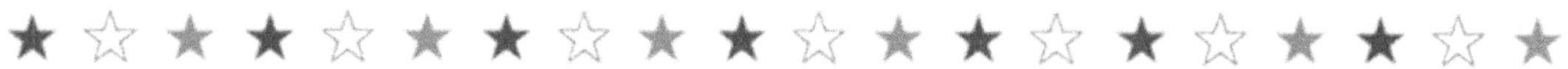

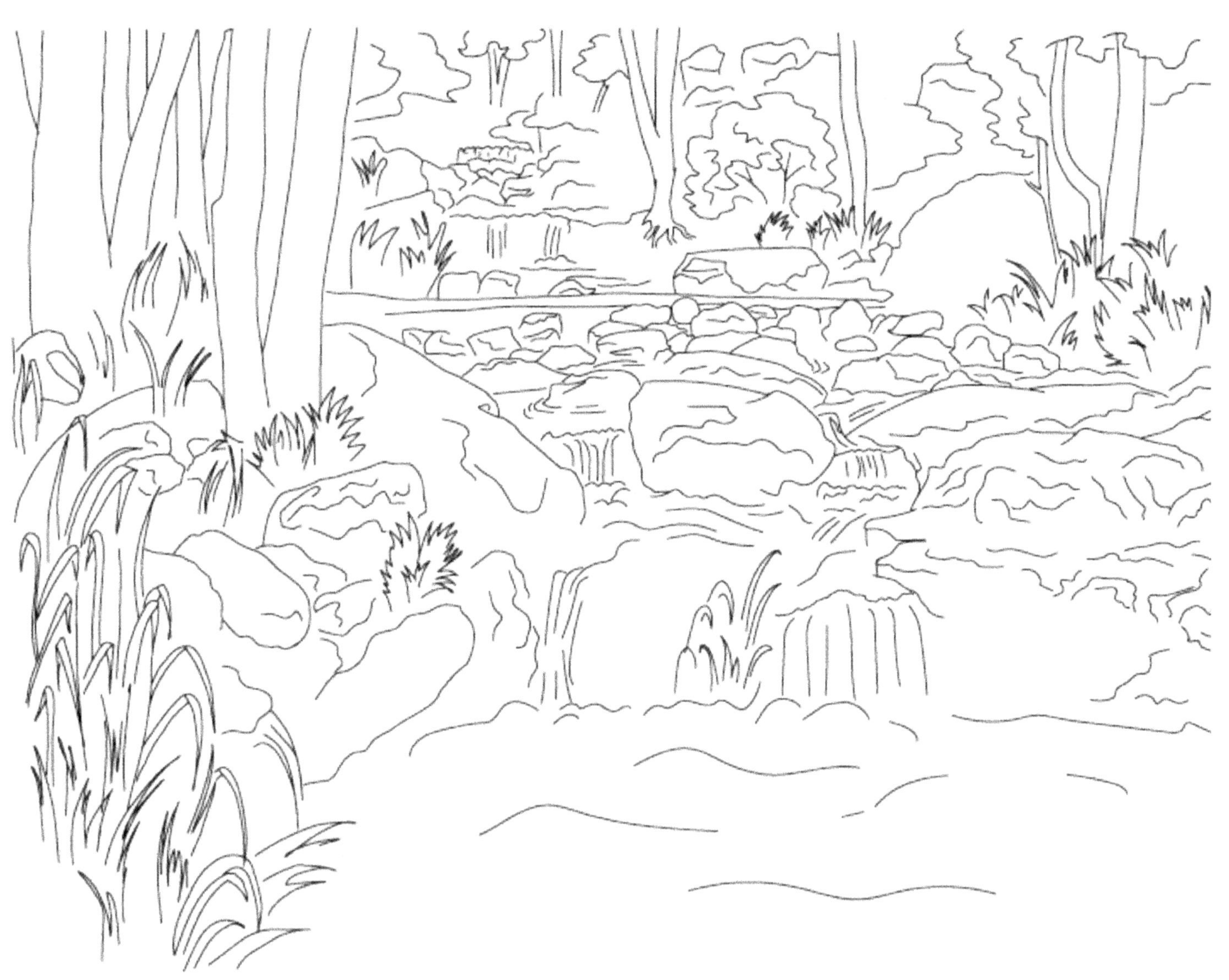

Doll Baby Trailhead: A Scenic Gateway in Arizona

Shaded by the majestic trees of the Tonto National Forest, the Doll Baby Trailhead near Payson, Arizona, offers access to several scenic trails, making it a popular spot for hikers and outdoor enthusiasts.

Trail Overview

Length Varies based on chosen routes
Difficulty: Moderate to challenging
Elevation Gain: Varies
Best Time to Visit: Spring through Fall

The trailhead is easily accessible from Payson, starting with a drive along Main Street, which becomes Country Club Drive and then Doll Baby Ranch Road. This route takes you through beautiful forested areas and along the East Verde River, providing a serene hiking experience. Some highlights include your ability to enjoy views of the Mazatzal Wilderness and the Mogollon Rim. A bit of historical interest, the trail passes near historical sites such as the Cracker Jack Mine ruins.

Fun Facts

Doll Baby Ranch: The trailhead is named after the historic Doll Baby Ranch, a landmark in the area known for its picturesque scenery and historical significance.

Open Range Land, the trail traverses open range land, where hikers might encounter free-roaming cattle, a common sight in this region of Arizona.

Navigation: The trail can be tricky to follow in places, so a reliable map or GPS is recommended.

The Doll Baby Trailhead provides a perfect starting point for exploring the natural beauty of the Tonto National Forest, offering a mix of historical interest, scenic views, and outdoor adventure.

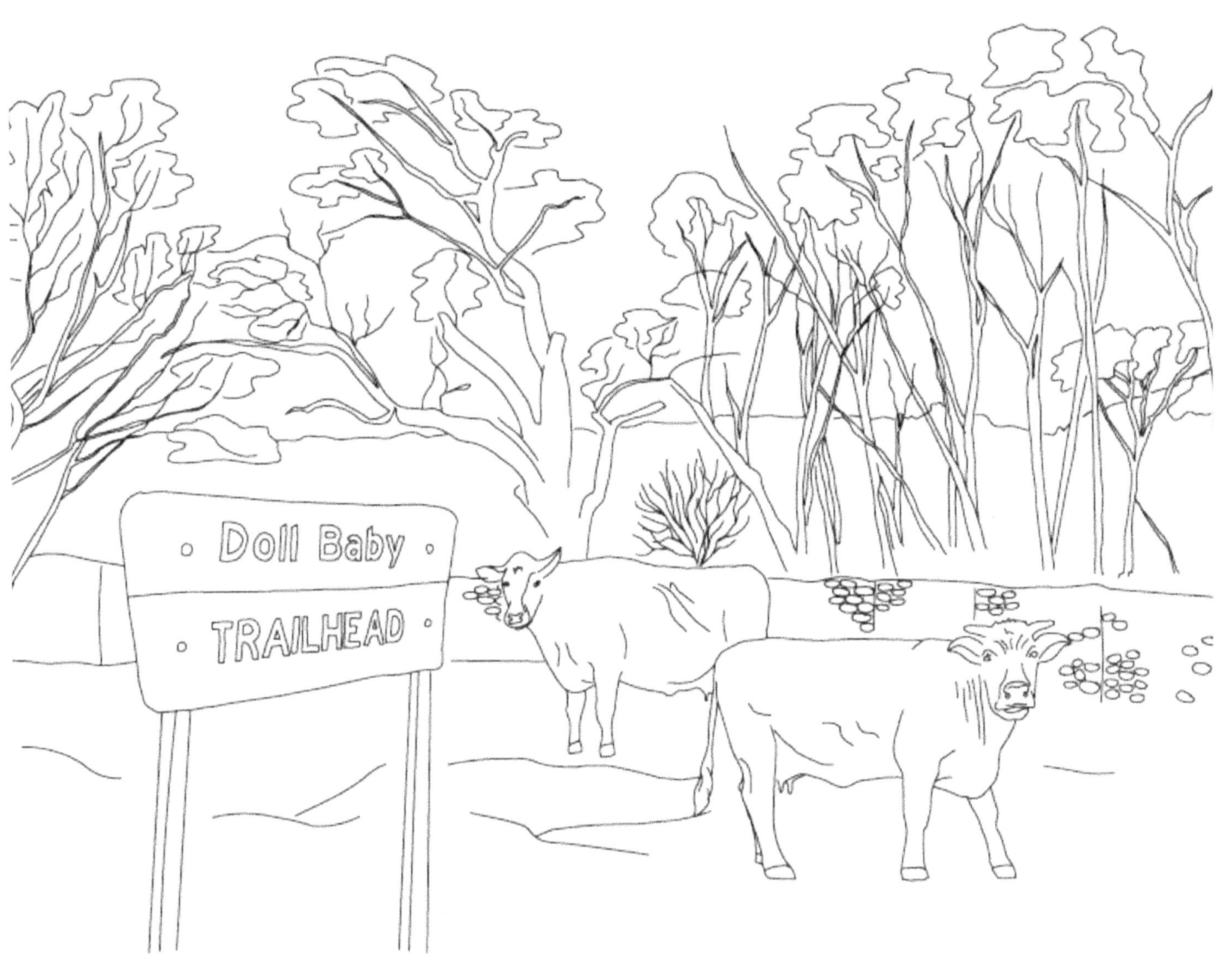
Doll Baby
TRAILHEAD

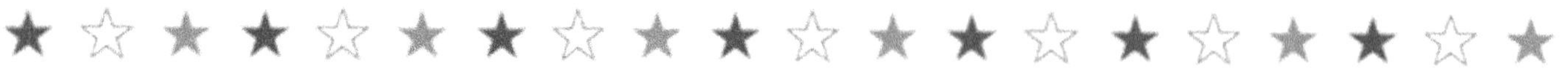

Houston Loop Trail: A Serene Hike in Payson, Arizona

Shaded by the lush pine forests of the Tonto National Forest, the **Houston Loop Trail** near Payson, Arizona, offers a peaceful and moderately challenging hiking experience. This loop trail is known for its tranquility, providing a peaceful retreat from the hustle and bustle of everyday life and showcases the natural beauty of the region, making it a favorite among hikers, mountain bikers, and equestrians.

Trail Overview

Length 4.3 miles round trip from the Mayfield Canyon Road trailhead
Difficulty : Moderate
Elevation Gain Approximately 300 feet
Best Time to Visit* Spring through Fall

The trail is easily accessible from Payson. To reach the trailhead, take HWY 87 North towards Payson, then HWY 260 east toward Star Valley. Turn left onto Mayfield Canyon Road and follow the signs to the Houston Loop trailhead.

Tips for Hikers

Parking: Parking can be challenging near the trailhead. If no spots are available, consider parking at the nearby dog park and walking to the trail.

Fun Facts

Historical Significance: The trail runs through areas historically used for ranching and mining, adding a touch of historical interest to the hike.

Diverse Ecosystem: The forested area is home to a wide variety of plant species, including ponderosa pines and scrub oak, creating a rich and diverse ecosystem

Wildlife Safety: Bear scat has been reported on the trail, so consider bringing bear spray and hiking in a group if concerned about encounters with wildlife.

The Houston Loop Trail offers a delightful mix of natural beauty, moderate challenge, and serene environment, making it an excellent choice for outdoor enthusiasts visiting the Payson area.

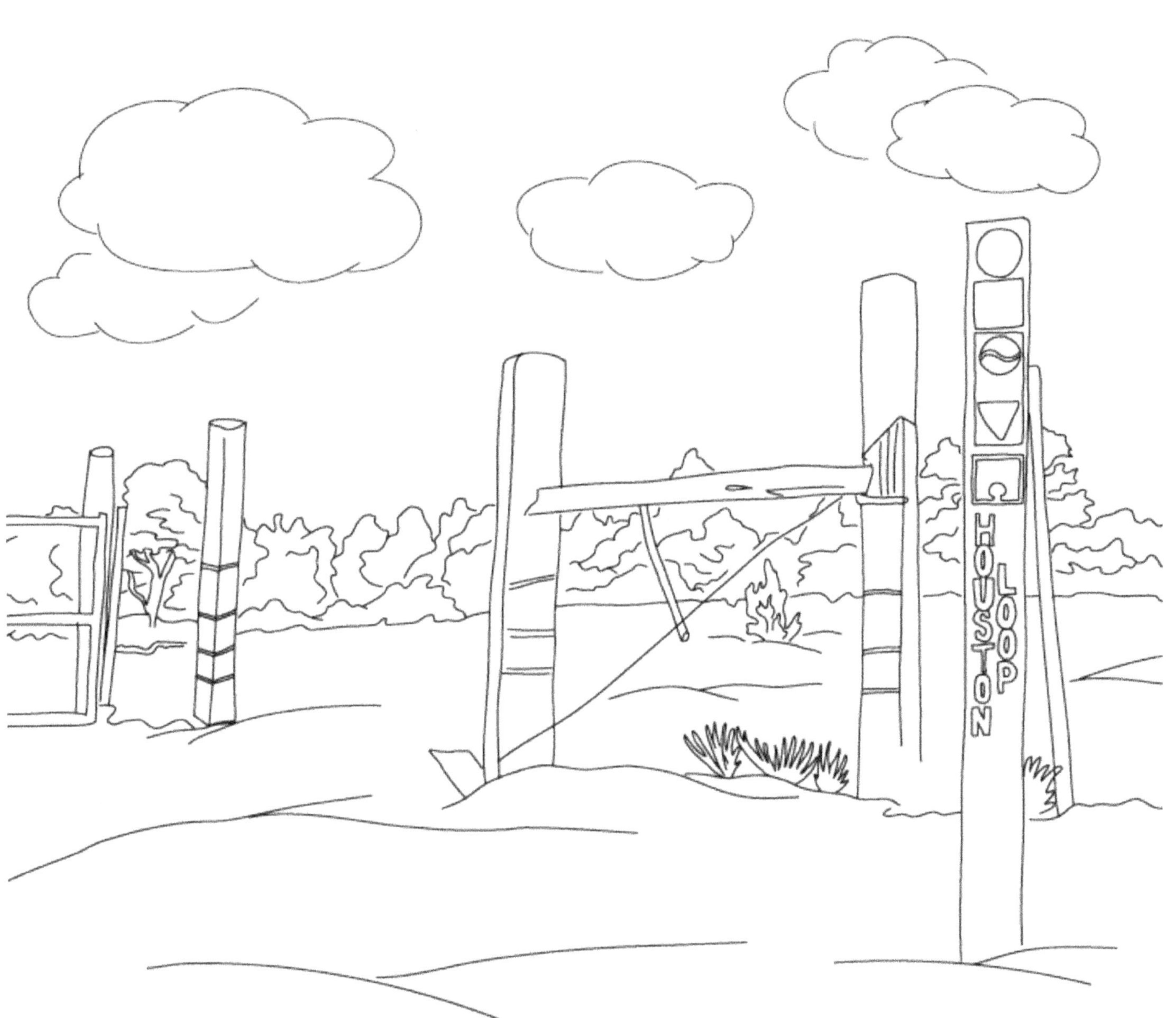

HOUSTON
LOOP

Tonto Natural Bridge: A Geological Marvel in Arizona

Tonto Natural Bridge State Park is a stunning natural wonder located near Payson, Arizona. This park is home to the world's largest natural travertine bridge, a remarkable formation that has attracted visitors from around the globe.

This impressive bridge is formed from travertine, a type of limestone deposited by mineral springs. The bridge spans Pine Creek, creating a beautiful natural tunnel below.

Trails and Activities

Pine Creek Trail* A half-mile trail that leads to the bottom of the bridge. It includes a mix of paved and rocky paths, some of which can be slippery.

Waterfall Trail* A short 300-foot trail ending at a waterfall cave. It's a quick but slightly challenging hike **due to uneven steps.**

Gowan Trail* This half-mile trail descends steeply to an observation deck beneath the bridge, offering a **fantastic view of the tunnel.**

Anna Mae Trail* A 500-foot trail connecting to Pine Creek Trail and leading to the bridge. Wildlife and Ecosystem: The park supports a diverse range of flora and fauna, including numerous bird species, small mammals, and a variety of plant life typical of the region's forested areas.

Fun Facts

Geological Formation: The bridge was formed over thousands of years by Pine Creek cutting through a deposit of calcium carbonate, creating the travertine structure seen today.

Historic Goodfellow Lodge: The park's visitor center, Goodfellow Lodge, offers exhibits on the history of the bridge, its geological formation, and the area's prehistoric inhabitants.
Wildlife and Ecosystem: The park supports a diverse range of flora and fauna, including numerous bird species, small mammals, and a variety of plant life typical of the region's forested areas.

Tonto Natural Bridge State Park is a must-visit destination for anyone interested in geology, natural beauty, and outdoor adventure. Whether you're hiking the trails, marveling at the bridge, or enjoying a picnic, this park provides a memorable experience in the heart of Arizona.

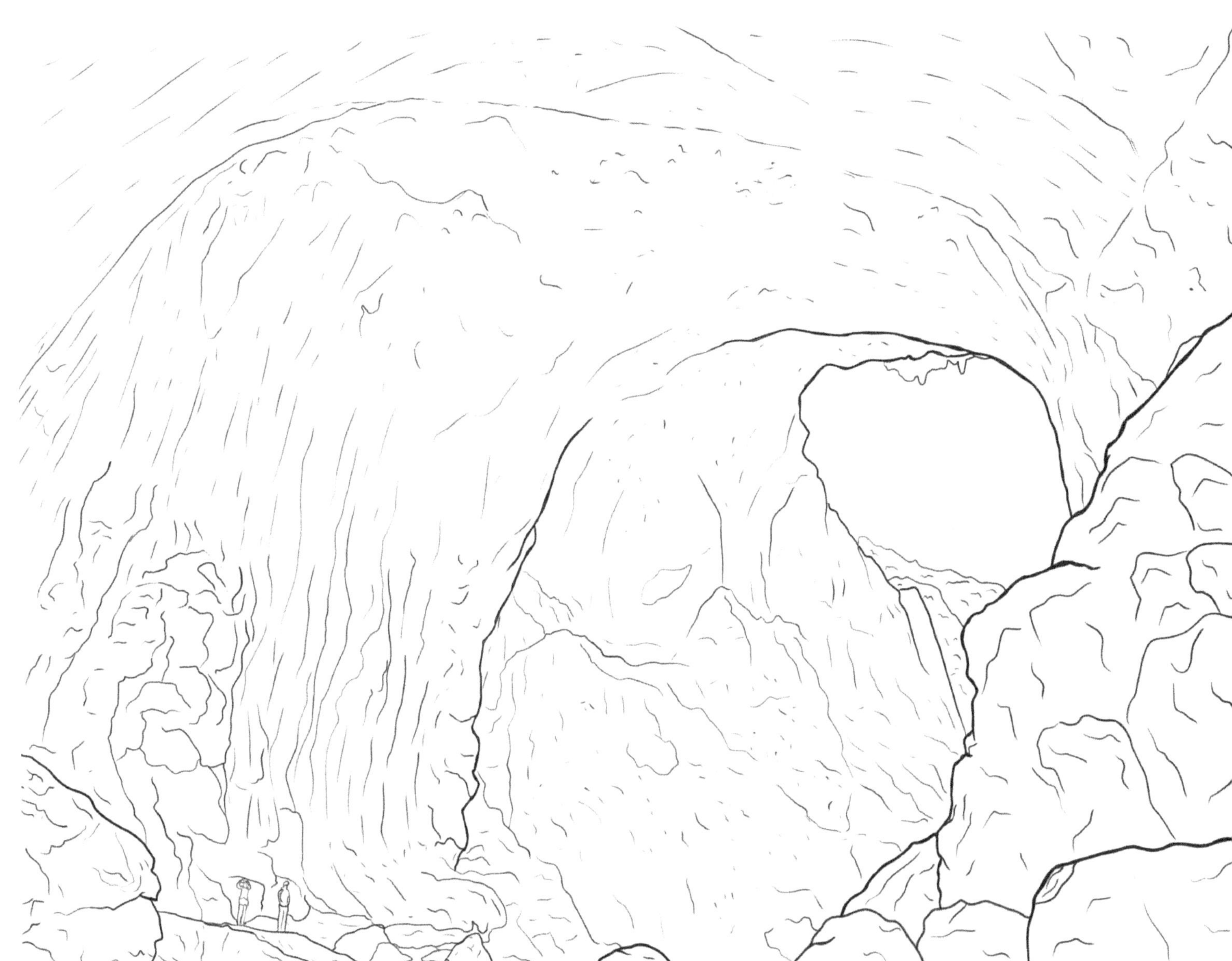

Christopher Creek: A Serene Retreat in Arizona

Nestled in the lush Tonto National Forest, Christopher Creekoffers a picturesque and tranquil escape, perfect for outdoor enthusiasts and nature lovers. The creek, fed by spring water, winds through the forest, providing a serene backdrop for various recreational activities.

Key Features

Christopher Creek is located near the Mogollon Rim, about 21 miles east of Payson, Arizona. The area is accessible via Highway 260, making it an easy drive from Payson.

Elevation: At over 5,600 feet above sea level, the area enjoys cool, crisp mountain air and stunning views of the surrounding forest and the Mogollon Rim.

Woods Canyon Lake: A short drive from Christopher Creek, this popular lake offers boating, fishing, and a nature trail around its perimeter.

Fun Facts

Historical Significance: The area around Christopher Creek has been a popular retreat for many years and was even featured in Zane Grey's Western novels. The creek and its surroundings have inspired many with their natural beauty and tranquility.

Christopher Creek provides a peaceful and scenic destination for anyone looking to enjoy the great outdoors in Arizona. Whether you're fishing in the clear waters, hiking along forest trails, or simply relaxing by the creek, it offers a perfect getaway from the hustle and bustle of everyday life.

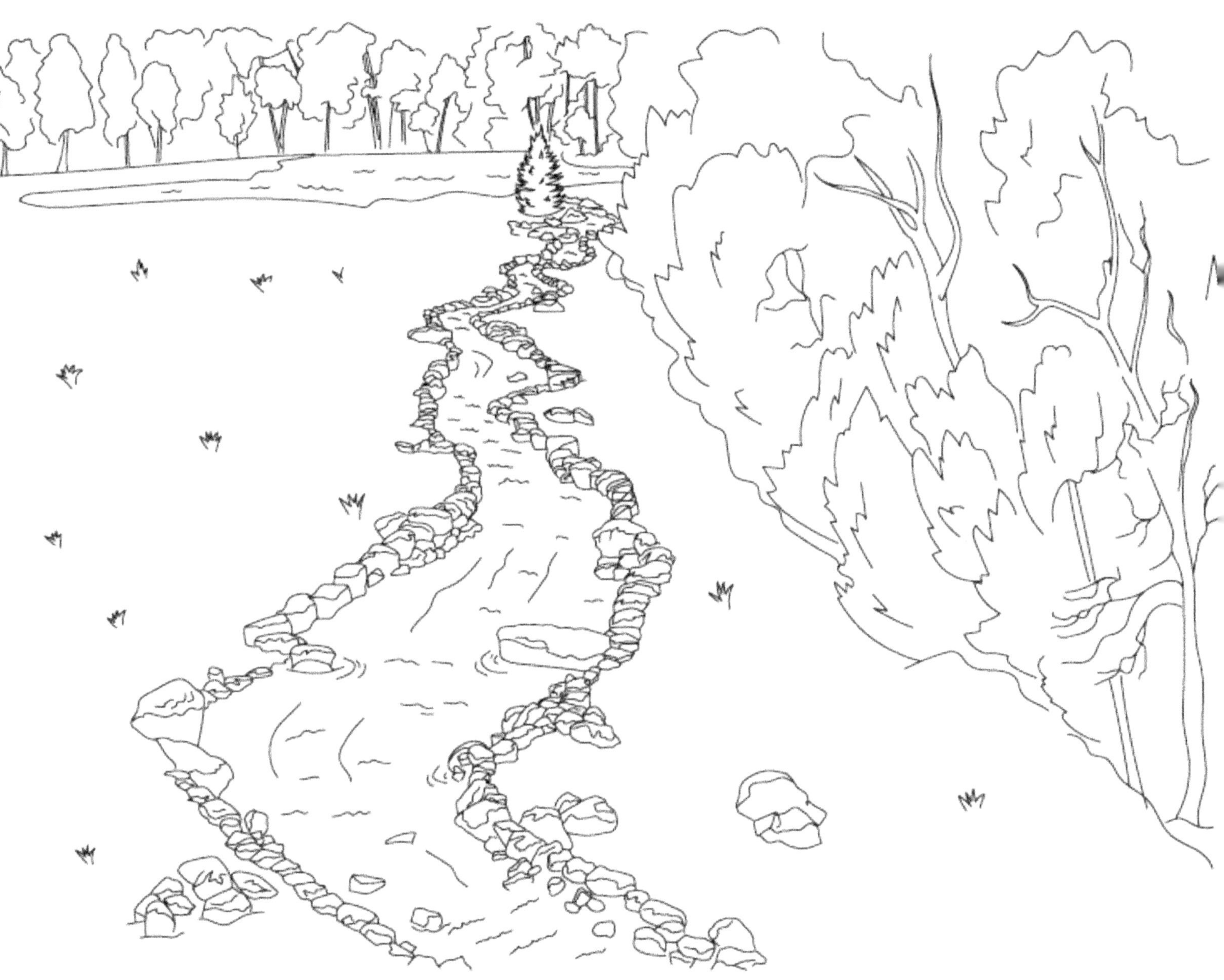

Woods Canyon Lake: An Oasis in Arizona's Rim Country

Nestled in the Apache-Sitgreaves National Forests, **Woods Canyon Lake** is a breathtaking gem located atop the Mogollon Rim in Arizona. This high-elevation lake offers a serene and picturesque retreat for outdoor enthusiasts, featuring crystal-clear waters surrounded by lush pine forests.

Situated at an elevation of approximately 7,510 feet, Woods Canyon Lake is just a short drive from Payson, Arizona, via Highway 260. The lake is easily accessible and provides a cool escape from the desert heat below. The lake spans about 55 acres, providing ample space for various water-based activities.

Woods Canyon Lake is a popular destination for anglers. The lake is regularly stocked with rainbow trout by the Arizona Game and Fish Department, making it a prime spot for fishing. Anglers can also find other species such as brown trout and largemouth bass.

Non-motorized boats and electric motor boats are allowed on the lake, offering a peaceful way to explore the water. Canoes, kayaks, and paddleboats can be rented at the nearby marina.

A scenic nature trail loops around the lake, providing stunning views of the water and surrounding forest. The trail is relatively easy and suitable for hikers of all skill levels.

The area around Woods Canyon Lake is rich with wildlife.

Fun Facts

Geological Marvel: The lake is situated on the Mogollon Rim, a 200-mile-long escarpment that offers dramatic views and unique geological features. The rim itself was formed by faulting and erosion over the years.

Visitors may spot elk, deer, bald eagles, and various bird species as they explore the area.

The Woods Canyon Lake area boasts several campgrounds, offering both developed and primitive camping options. These campgrounds are equipped with amenities such as picnic tables, fire rings, and restrooms, making it a convenient spot for an extended stay.

Whether you're casting a line into its clear waters, hiking through the towering pines, or simply relaxing by the shore, Woods Canyon Lake offers a peaceful and scenic escape that showcases the natural beauty of Arizona's Rim Country.

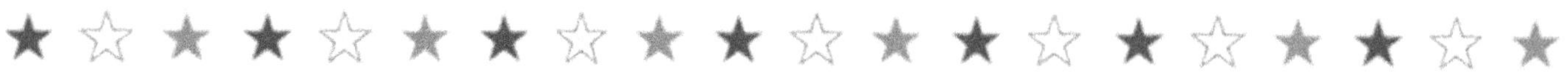

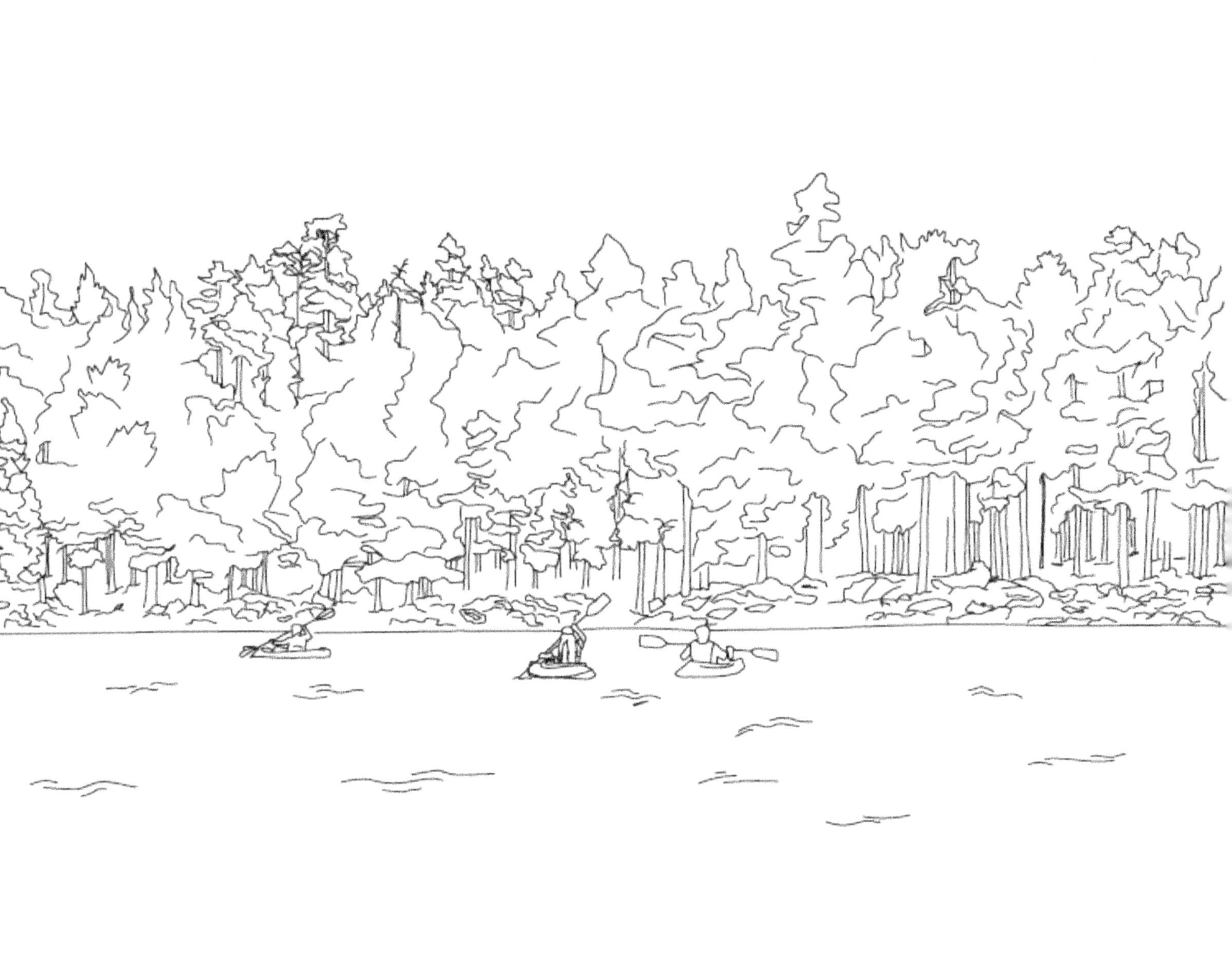

The Mogollon Rim: Arizona's Majestic Escarpment

Stretching across central Arizona, the Mogollon Rim is one of the state's most spectacular and defining geological features. This massive escarpment forms a dramatic boundary between the Colorado Plateau to the north and the Basin and Range region to the south, offering breathtaking vistas, rich history, and a diverse range of outdoor activities.

The Mogollon Rim was formed over millions of years through a combination of faulting, volcanic activity, and erosion. The result is a steep, rugged cliff that rises up to 2,000 feet in some places and extends for over 200 miles across Arizona. Composed primarily of limestone, sandstone, and basalt, the rim showcases layers of sedimentary rock that date back to the Paleozoic Era, revealing a fascinating geological history.

The rim offers some of the most stunning panoramic views in the Southwest. From its highest points, visitors can gaze out over vast forests of ponderosa pine, deep canyons, and expansive plateaus. Popular viewpoints include the Rim Road (Forest Road 300) and the Mogollon Rim Visitor Center. The area is covered by lush forests that provide habitat for a wide variety of wildlife, including elk, black bears, mountain lions, and numerous bird species. The mix of pine, fir, and aspen trees creates a vibrant and diverse ecosystem.

Fun Facts

The name "Mogollon" is derived from Don Juan Ignacio Flores Mogollón, a Spanish colonial governor of New Mexico in the early 18th century. Due to its high elevation and clear skies, the Mogollon Rim is also a popular spot for stargazing and astronomical observation. The dark skies provide an excellent opportunity to observe celestial events without the interference of city lights.

The Mogollon Rim is a hiker's paradise with trails ranging from easy walks to challenging backcountry routes. Notable trails include the Highline Trail, which runs along the base of the rim, and the General Crook Trail, which offers historical insights along with natural beauty. The rim is dotted with numerous lakes and streams that are popular for fishing.

Whether you're an avid outdoor adventurer, a history buff, or simply someone who appreciates breathtaking natural beauty, the Mogollon Rim offers something for everyone. Its combination of geological wonder, rich biodiversity, and cultural significance makes it a must-visit destination in Arizona.

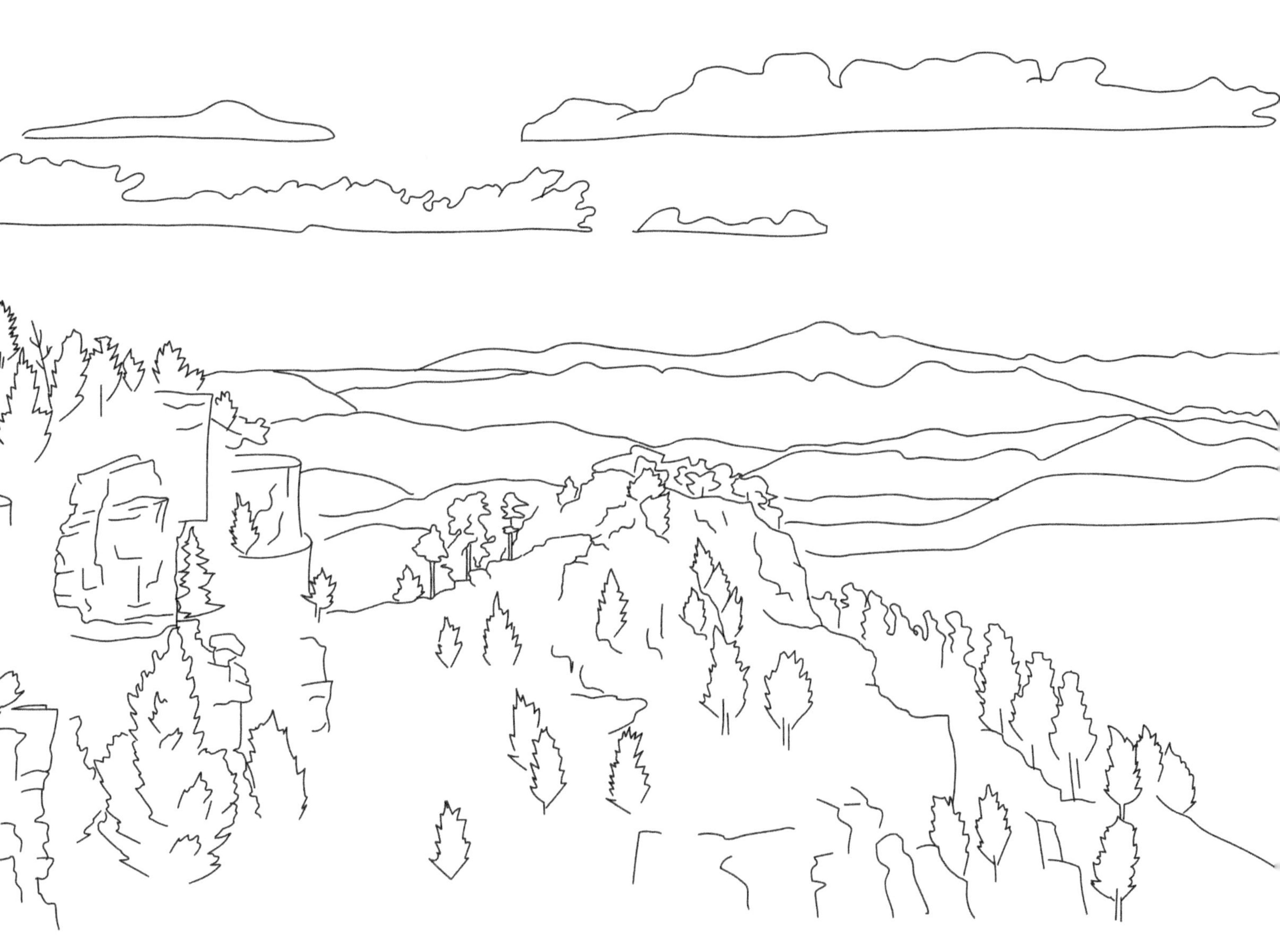

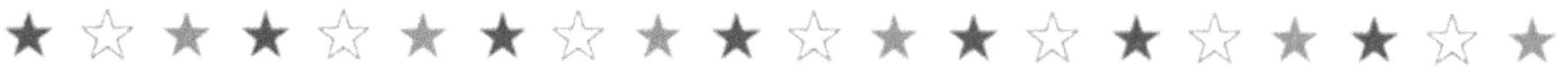

Woods Canyon Lake as an eagle breeding sanctuary

Woods Canyon Lake, nestled in the Mogollon Rim country of Arizona, is not only a scenic destination for outdoor enthusiasts but also serves as an important eagle breeding sanctuary. This role adds another layer of significance to the lake's already rich ecosystem.

Bald eagles, with their distinctive white heads and tails contrasting against dark brown bodies, have chosen Woods Canyon Lake as one of their nesting sites. These majestic birds, once endangered, have made a remarkable recovery, partly thanks to protected areas like this.

The lake's abundant fish population, particularly trout, provides an ideal food source for the eagles. The tall ponderosa pines surrounding the lake offer perfect nesting spots, allowing the eagles to build their massive nests high above the ground where they can safely raise their young.

During the breeding season, typically from December to June, visitors might spot eagles soaring over the lake, diving for fish, or perched regally in the treetops. However, it's crucial to observe from a distance to avoid disturbing these protected birds.

To protect the eagles, certain areas of the lake may have restricted access during the breeding season. These conservation efforts, supported by the Arizona Game and Fish Department and the U.S. Forest Service, have been crucial in maintaining a healthy eagle population.

Fun fact:

Bald eagle nests are among the largest of any North American bird, often measuring 4-5 feet wide and 2-4 feet deep. These nests can weigh up to a ton and are often reused and added to year after year.

The presence of breeding bald eagles at Woods Canyon Lake is a testament to the area's ecological health and the success of wildlife conservation efforts. It adds an extra element of wonder for visitors, who might be lucky enough to witness these magnificent birds in their natural habitat.

Whether you're an avid birdwatcher or simply a nature enthusiast, the knowledge that Woods Canyon Lake plays a vital role in eagle conservation adds depth to the experience of visiting this beautiful Arizona landmark.

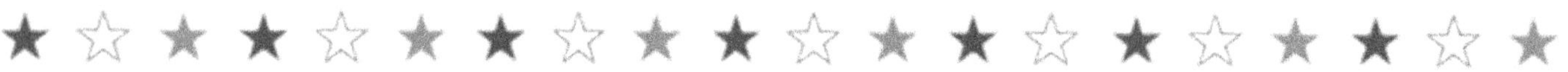

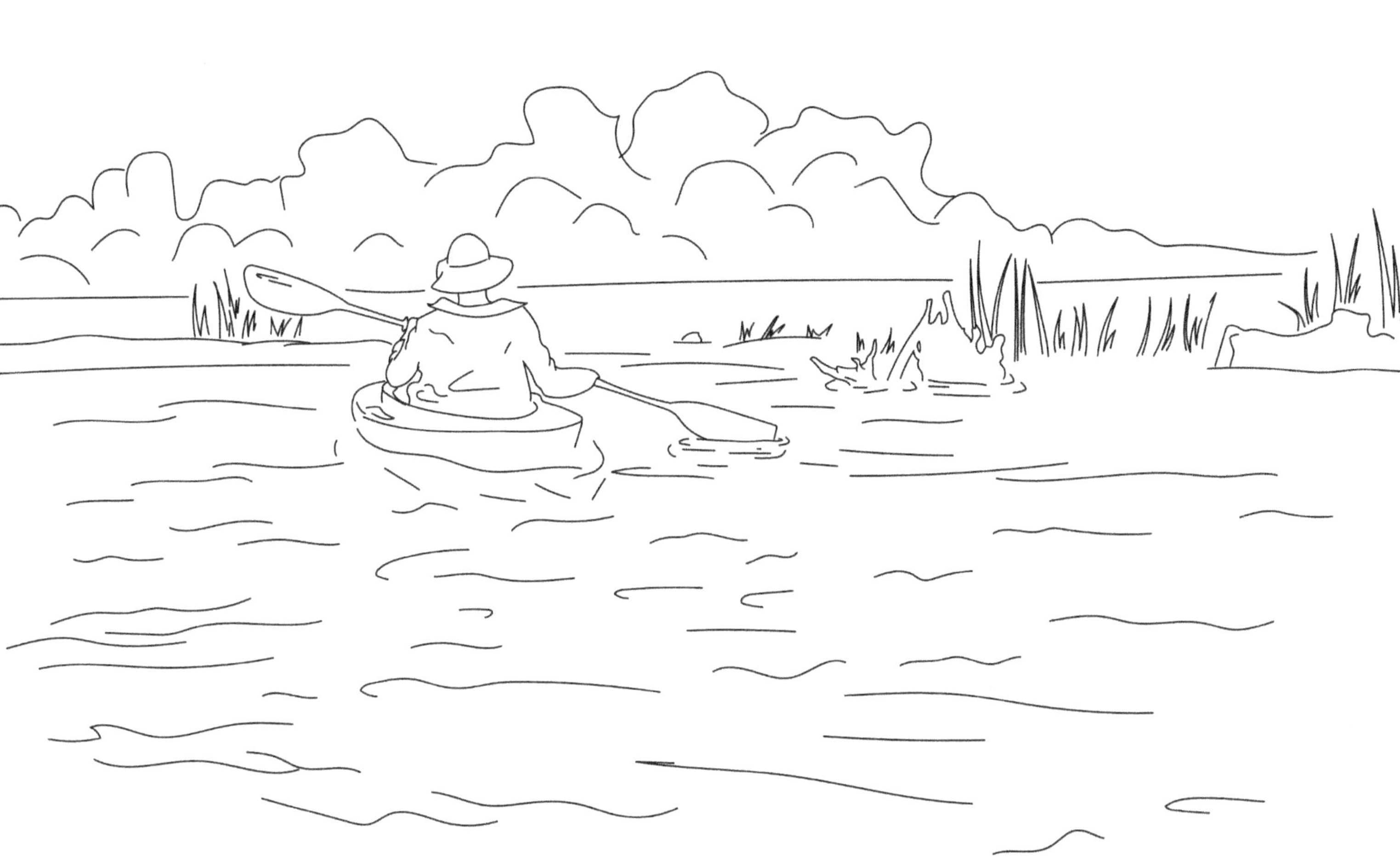

Hiking opportunities around Woods Canyon Lake:

The main trail at Woods Canyon Lake is the Woods Canyon Lake Trail, a 5.5-mile loop that encircles the entire lake. This trail offers hikers a variety of experiences:

1. Difficulty: The trail is generally considered easy to moderate, making it accessible for most hikers, including families with children.

2. Terrain: The path winds through ponderosa pine forest, occasionally opening up to provide stunning views of the lake. It includes some gentle elevation changes but nothing too strenuous.

3. Points of Interest: Along the way, hikers can enjoy several scenic overlooks, rocky outcroppings, and quiet coves perfect for wildlife viewing.

4. Connectivity: The Woods Canyon Lake Trail connects to other trails in the area, including:
   - The Rim Lake Vista Trail: This 3.5-mile trail offers spectacular views of the Mogollon Rim.
   - The Springs Trail: A 2-mile out-and-back trail that leads to a series of small springs.

5. Seasonal Variations: In spring and summer, wildflowers dot the landscape. Fall brings beautiful changing colors to the aspen trees. Winter transforms the area into a snowy wonderland, though some trails may be less accessible.

Fun fact:

The area around Woods Canyon Lake is part of the larger Rim Lakes Recreation Area, which offers over 50 miles of interconnected trails. Ambitious hikers can create longer routes by combining multiple trails.

Remember that trail conditions can vary depending on recent weather and the time of year. It's always a good idea to check with the local ranger station for the most up-to-date information before setting out on a hike.

Whether you're looking for a short stroll or a full day's adventure, the trails around Woods Canyon Lake offer beautiful scenery and a chance to immerse yourself in Arizona's high country wilderness.

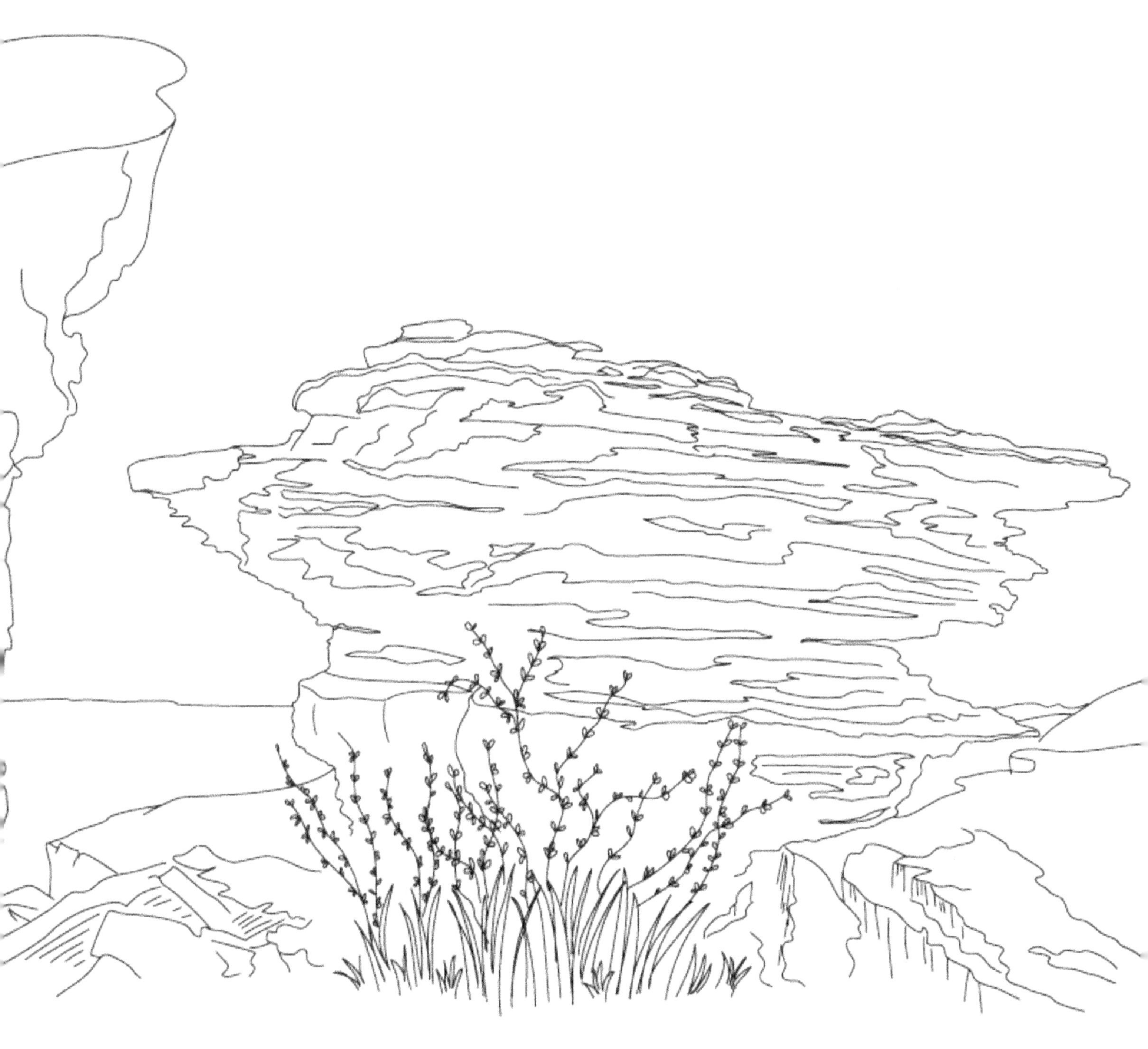

Sunflowers

The Sunflower (Helianthus annuus) is a striking sight in Arizona's landscape, with its large, golden blooms reaching towards the sky. These native North American plants can grow impressively tall, sometimes reaching heights of over 16 feet. Their bright yellow petals surround a dark center filled with seeds, creating a beautiful contrast.

Sunflowers are more than just pretty faces in the garden. They play a crucial role in Arizona's ecosystem, providing food and shelter for various wildlife. Birds, bees, and butterflies are frequent visitors, drawn to the nectar and pollen of these magnificent flowers.

> *Fun fact:*
>
> Sunflowers are nature's sun trackers! Young sunflower heads exhibit a behavior called heliotropism, where they follow the sun's movement across the sky from east to west during the day. At night, they slowly turn back east to greet the morning sun. This "sun dance" stops once the flowers mature and permanently face east.

In Arizona, sunflowers typically bloom from late summer to early fall, adding a burst of color to the landscape as other plants begin to fade. Their presence is a cheerful reminder of the changing seasons in the desert state.

These versatile plants have been cultivated for thousands of years, valued for their seeds, oil, and ornamental beauty. Today, they continue to be an important crop and a beloved garden flower throughout Arizona and beyond.

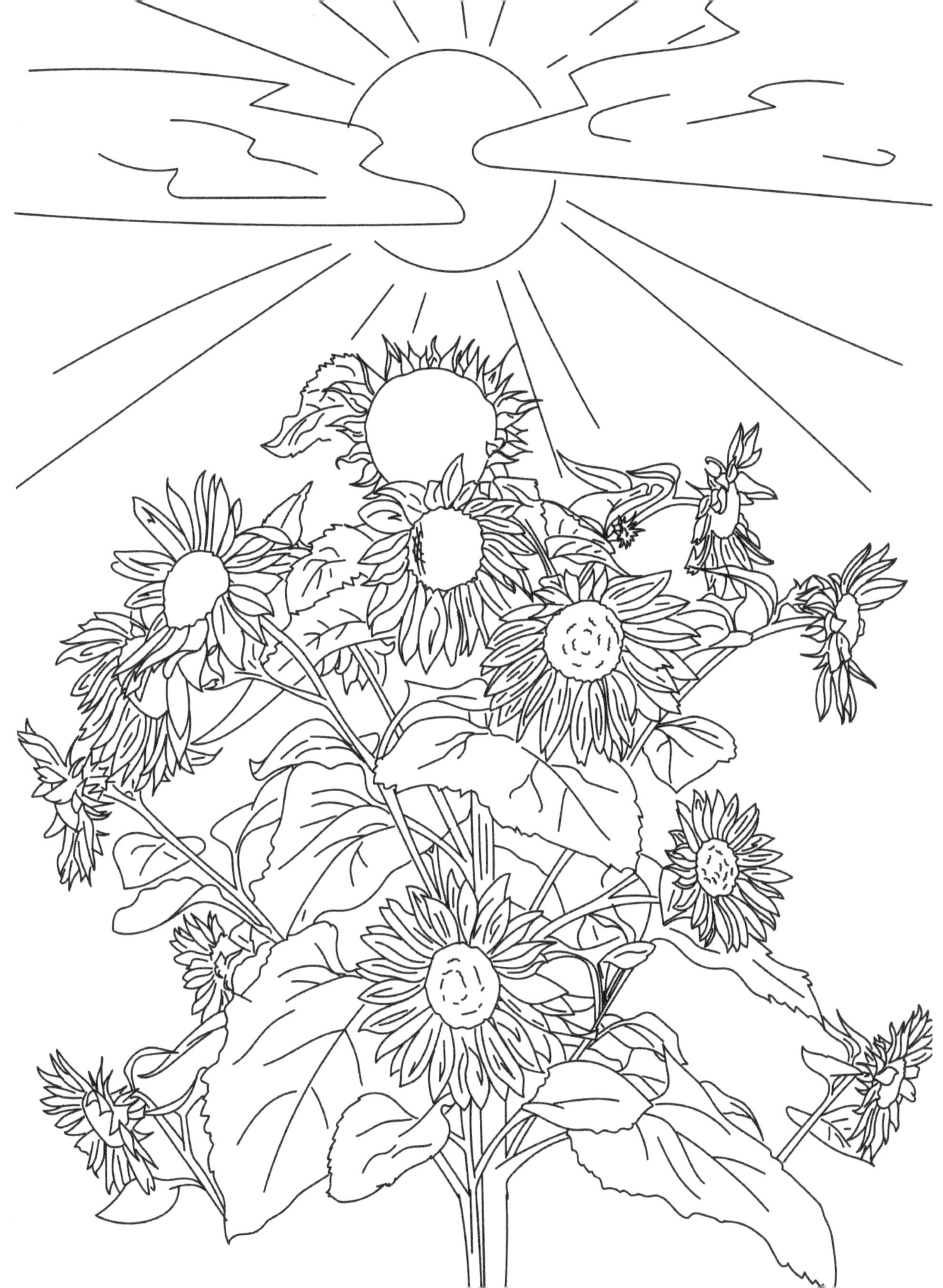

The Mountain Lion (Puma concolor), also known as the cougar or puma, is Arizona's largest wild cat. These powerful and sleek predators can be found throughout the state's diverse landscapes, from the high forests to the low deserts.

Adult mountain lions typically measure 6-8 feet long from nose to tail tip and can weigh between 80-150 pounds, with males generally larger than females. Their coat is a tawny golden-brown color, helping them blend seamlessly into Arizona's rocky and forested terrains.

These solitary and elusive cats are known for their strength and agility. They can leap up to 40 feet horizontally and 15 feet vertically, making them exceptional hunters. Mountain lions primarily prey on deer, but they're opportunistic and will also hunt smaller mammals and even reptiles.

Fun fact:

Despite their large size, mountain lions cannot roar like lions or tigers. Instead, they communicate through a variety of vocalizations including purrs, chirps, whistles, and even screams. Their most distinctive sound is a high-pitched scream that some describe as similar to a woman's scream, which has led to various folklore tales in Arizona's history.

Mountain lions play a crucial role in maintaining ecological balance in Arizona's ecosystems. As apex predators, they help control deer populations and influence the behavior of other species in their habitat.

While rarely seen by humans due to their secretive nature, the mountain lion remains an iconic symbol of the wild and untamed beauty of Arizona's natural landscapes.

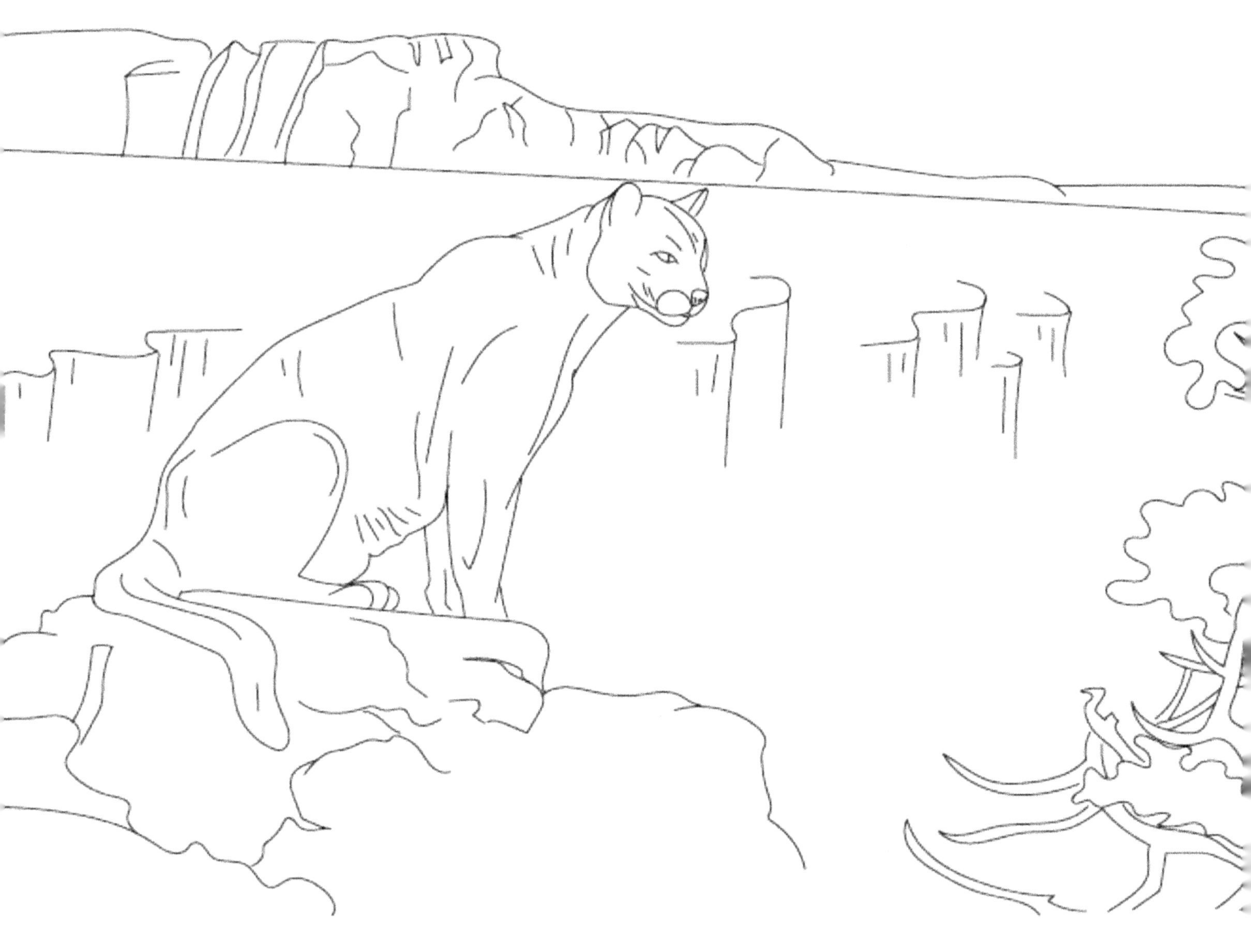

Javelinas

Javelinas, while pig-like in appearance, are actually more closely related to hippopotamuses than to true pigs. Both javelinas and hippos belong to the order Artiodactyla, sharing a distant common ancestor, though the exact timing of their evolutionary divergence is still a subject of scientific study."

Javelinas are social animals, typically living in herds of 8-12 individuals. They're primarily herbivorous, feeding on cacti, roots, tubers, and other vegetation, but they'll occasionally eat small animals or eggs if the opportunity arises. This diverse diet is another trait they share with hippos, who are also omnivores despite being primarily plant-eaters.

These fascinating creatures play an important role in the Arizona ecosystem, helping to disperse seeds and control vegetation growth in their habitats. Their presence in the Americas, along with their hippo relatives in Africa, showcases the diverse evolutionary paths of these related species.

Fun fact:

Like their distant hippo cousins, Javelinas have a unique way of marking their territory and communicating with each other. They have a scent gland on their backs that releases a musky odor. Members of a herd will rub against each other to spread this scent, creating a "group smell" that helps them recognize members of their family group.

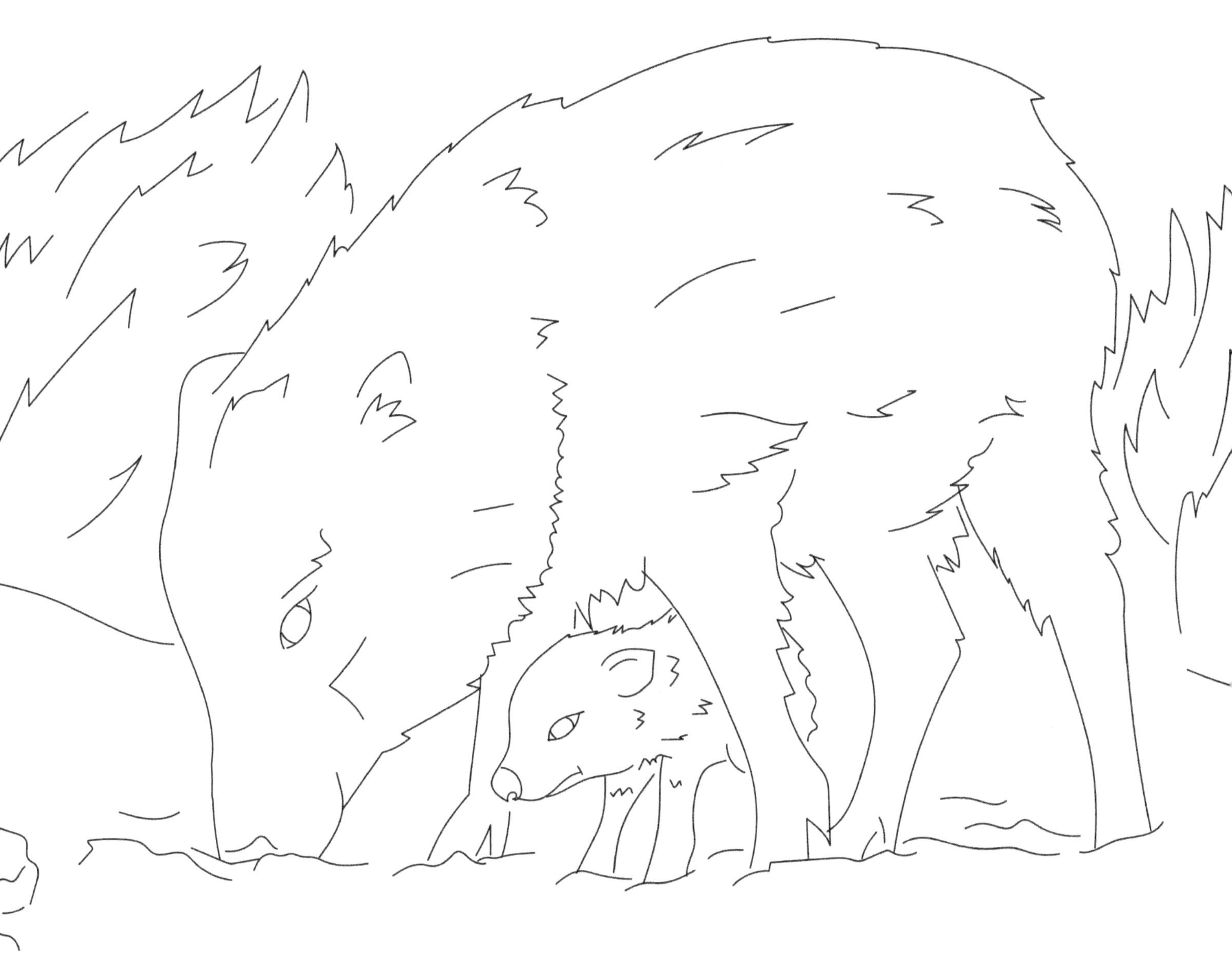

The Arizona Coyote: A Versatile Predator

The coyote (Canis latrans), commonly found throughout North America, is a resilient and adaptable predator that thrives in a variety of environments, including the diverse landscapes of Arizona. Known for their intelligence and versatility, coyotes play a crucial role in the ecosystem.

Coyotes typically weigh between 20 to 50 pounds and stand about 24 inches tall at the shoulder. They have a slender build with long legs, a narrow snout, and a bushy tail often tipped with black. Their fur is generally grayish-brown with reddish tinges behind the ears and around the face. The color can vary depending on the environment, providing camouflage in different terrains. Coyotes are highly adaptable and can be found in deserts, forests, grasslands, and urban areas. In Arizona, they inhabit regions from the Sonoran Desert to the pine forests of the Mogollon Rim. Individual territories can range from 10 to 40 square miles, depending on food availability and population density.

Coyotes are opportunistic feeders, with a diet that includes small mammals, birds, reptiles, insects, fruits, and carrion. They are also known to hunt in pairs or small family groups to take down larger prey like deer.
 They use a combination of stalking and pouncing to capture prey and are known for their cunning and strategic hunting methods.

Fun Facts

In Native American folklore, the coyote is often depicted as a trickster figure, embodying both cunning and survival skills.

Coyotes have expanded their range across North America, thriving in environments altered by human activity, unlike many other predators.

Coyotes are social animals that often live in family groups consisting of a breeding pair and their offspring. They communicate using a range of vocalizations, including howls, yips, and barks, which help maintain territory and social bonds.

Coyotes are a testament to nature's adaptability and resilience. Their presence in Arizona's varied landscapes highlights their role in maintaining ecological balance. Understanding and respecting these intelligent predators can lead to better coexistence and appreciation of the natural world.

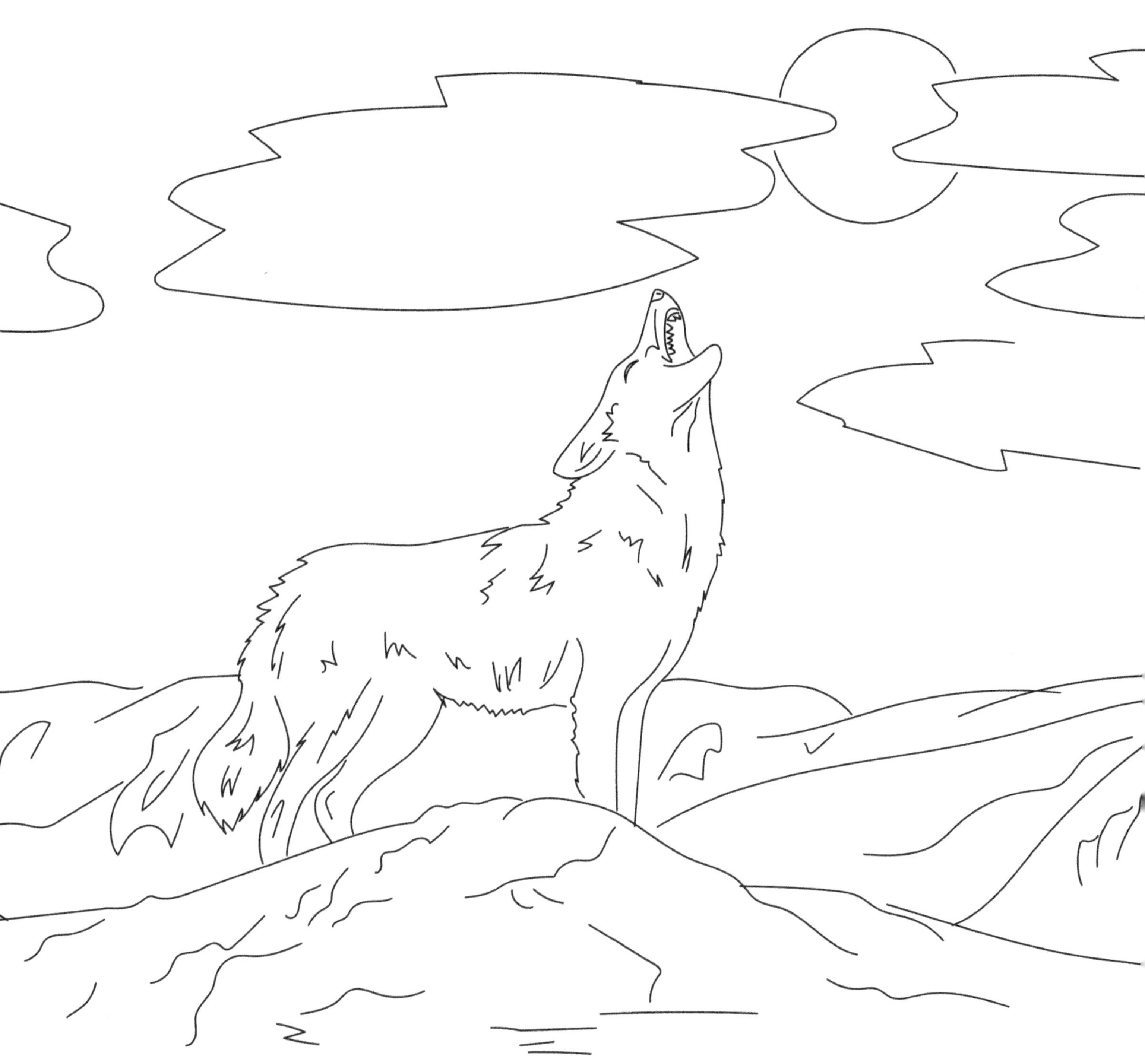

The Elk: A Local Legend in Payson, Arizona

The majestic Rocky Mountain Elk (Cervus canadensis nelsoni) is a prominent and beloved resident of Payson, Arizona, and the surrounding Mogollon Rim country. These impressive animals are a common sight in the area, often spotted grazing in meadows or moving through the ponderosa pine forests.

Elk are among the largest land mammals in North America, with bulls (males) weighing up to 700 pounds and standing 5 feet tall at the shoulder. Their reddish-brown coats and lighter-colored rumps make them stand out against the green backdrop of Payson's forests. Bulls are easily recognized by their massive antlers, which they shed and regrow annually.

Payson and its surrounding areas provide an ideal habitat for elk, with a mix of forest cover and open grasslands. The town itself has embraced its elk population, with many residents and visitors enjoying the frequent elk sightings in and around the community.

Fun fact:

During the fall rutting season, the haunting bugle calls of bull elk can be heard echoing through the canyons and forests around Payson. This eerie, high-pitched whistle is used to attract mates and challenge other bulls, creating one of nature's most impressive sound displays.

The elk population in the Payson area is not just a tourist attraction; it plays a crucial role in the local ecosystem. As large herbivores, elk help shape the landscape by influencing vegetation patterns through their grazing habits. They also serve as prey for predators like mountain lions, helping to maintain the balance of the food chain.

The Arizona Game and Fish Department closely manages the elk population to ensure its health and sustainability. Regulated hunting plays a role in this management, contributing to the local economy while helping to keep the elk population at a level the habitat can support.

Whether you're driving the scenic roads around Payson, hiking in the nearby forests, or even just walking through town, catching sight of these magnificent animals is a reminder of the wild beauty that makes Arizona so special.

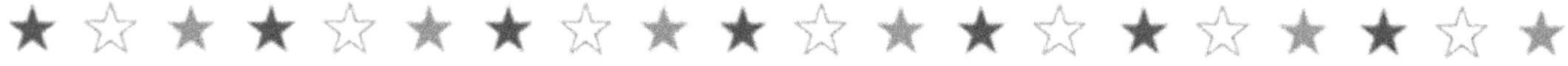

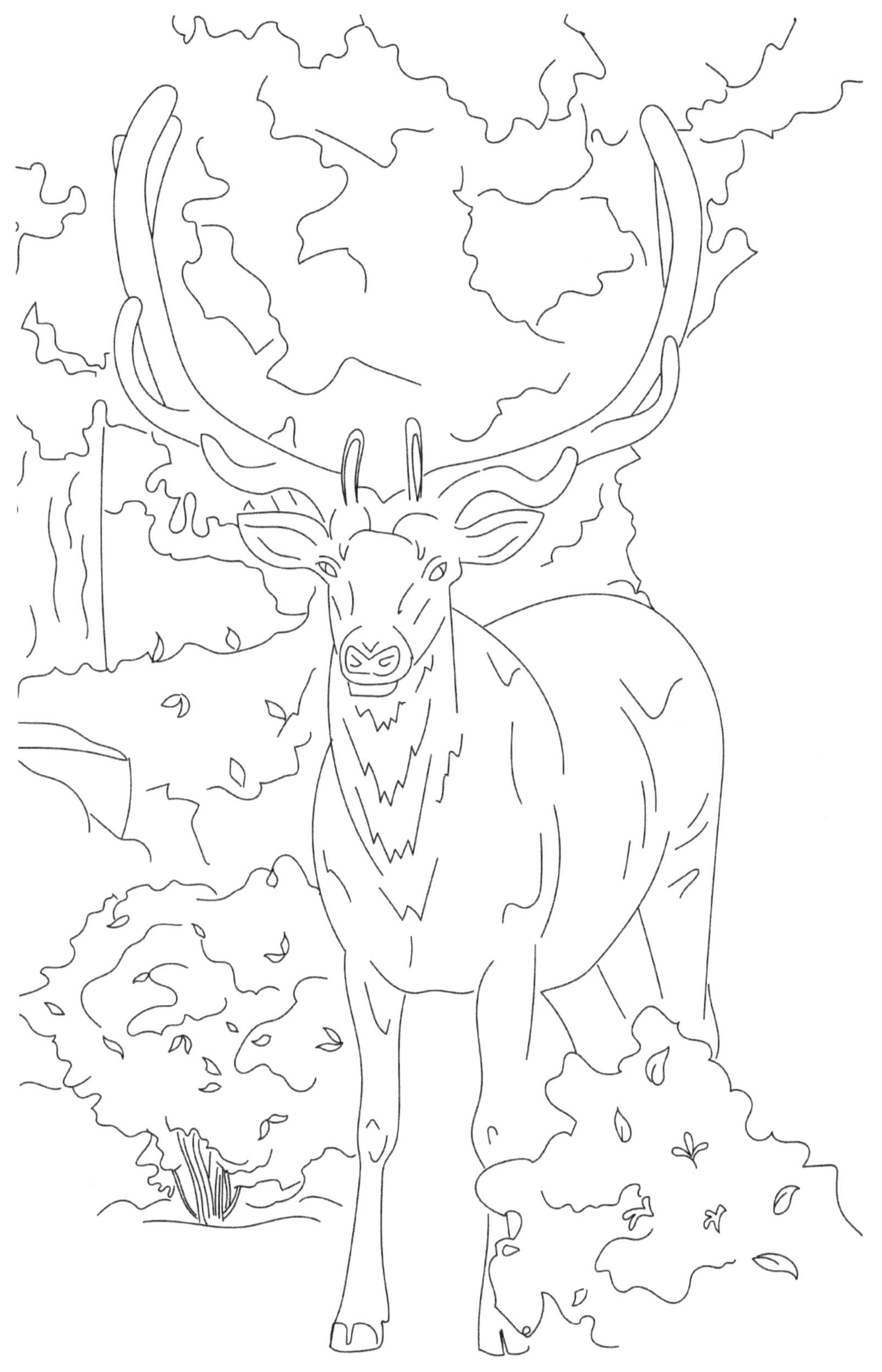

Black Bears in Rim Country, Arizona

The Mogollon Rim in Arizona, is home to a significant population of black bears. These bears thrive in the lush forests and diverse habitats of the region, making it an ideal spot for bear sightings and interactions with wildlife.

Black bears in Arizona vary in color, including black, brown, cinnamon, and dark blond. They typically weigh between 125 to 400 pounds, with males being larger than females. They stand 3 to 3.5 feet tall when on all fours and can reach 5 to 6 feet in length.

Their diet is primarily composed of acorns, berries, insects, and cactus fruits. They are omnivorous and opportunistic feeders, which sometimes leads them to human food sources.
Black bears are most active during dawn and dusk. In fall, they need to consume about 20,000 calories a day to build enough fat for hibernation during the winter months.

Rim Country provides an excellent habitat for black bears due to its dense forests and abundant food sources. The bears in this region are often seen around areas like Payson and Star Valley. Sightings tend to increase in late spring and early summer when juvenile bears leave their mothers and start exploring on their own.

Fun Facts:

Black bears can live up to 25 years in the wild.

When threatened or stressed, bears may make sounds such as woofing, hissing, teeth popping, and grunting.

Black bears generally avoid humans, but they can become problematic when they get accustomed to human food.

Understanding and respecting black bears is crucial for coexisting peacefully in Rim Country. By taking precautions and being mindful of their presence, residents and visitors can enjoy the natural beauty of this region while minimizing negative interactions with these magnificent creatures.

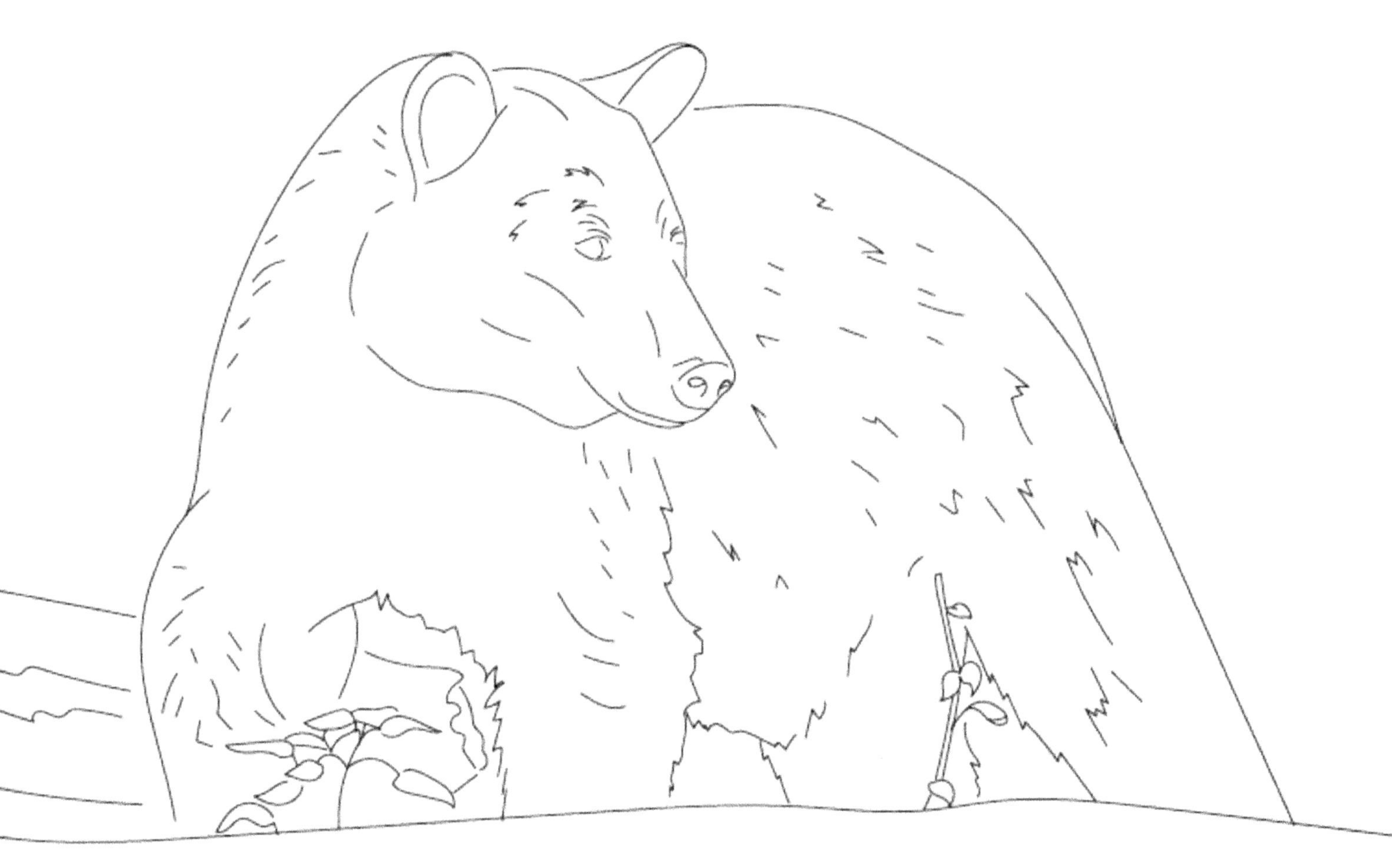

Arizona's State Insect: The Two-Tailed Swallowtail Butterfly

The two-tailed swallowtail butterfly,Papilio multicaudata, was designated as Arizona's official state butterfly in 2001. This beautiful butterfly is known for its striking appearance and is found primarily in the western United States, from southwestern Canada down to Mexico. The two-tailed swallowtail is one of the largest butterfly species in North America, boasting a wingspan of 3.5 to 5.5 inches. Its wings are bright yellow with black stripes running vertically along the forewings. The hindwings feature two distinctive tails, which give the butterfly its name. These hindwings also display blue patches and orange spots, adding to the butterfly's vibrant appearance. The caterpillar of the two-tailed swallowtail is light green with distinctive yellow dots and eye spots near the head.

This butterfly thrives in a variety of habitats, including canyons, foothills, valleys, woodlands, and even urban areas. They are commonly seen in Arizona's diverse landscapes, from the riparian zones to the high deserts. The two-tailed swallowtail's life cycle includes laying eggs on host plants like ash, hop tree, and chokecherry, which the caterpillars feed on. Adults are nectar feeders, often seen around thistles, milkweeds, and lilacs.

Fun Facts:

The two-tailed swallowtail is easily identified by the two tails on each hindwing, a unique feature among butterflies in the United States.

They are strong fliers and can be found from British Columbia to central Texas, demonstrating a wide adaptability to different climates and environments.

The two-tailed swallowtail butterfly not only adds beauty to Arizona's natural landscapes but also plays a crucial role in pollination. Its presence is a reminder of the state's rich biodiversity and the importance of preserving natural habitats. Whether spotted fluttering through canyons or gracing suburban gardens, this butterfly truly embodies the spirit of Arizona.

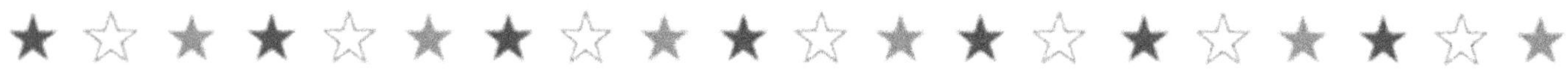

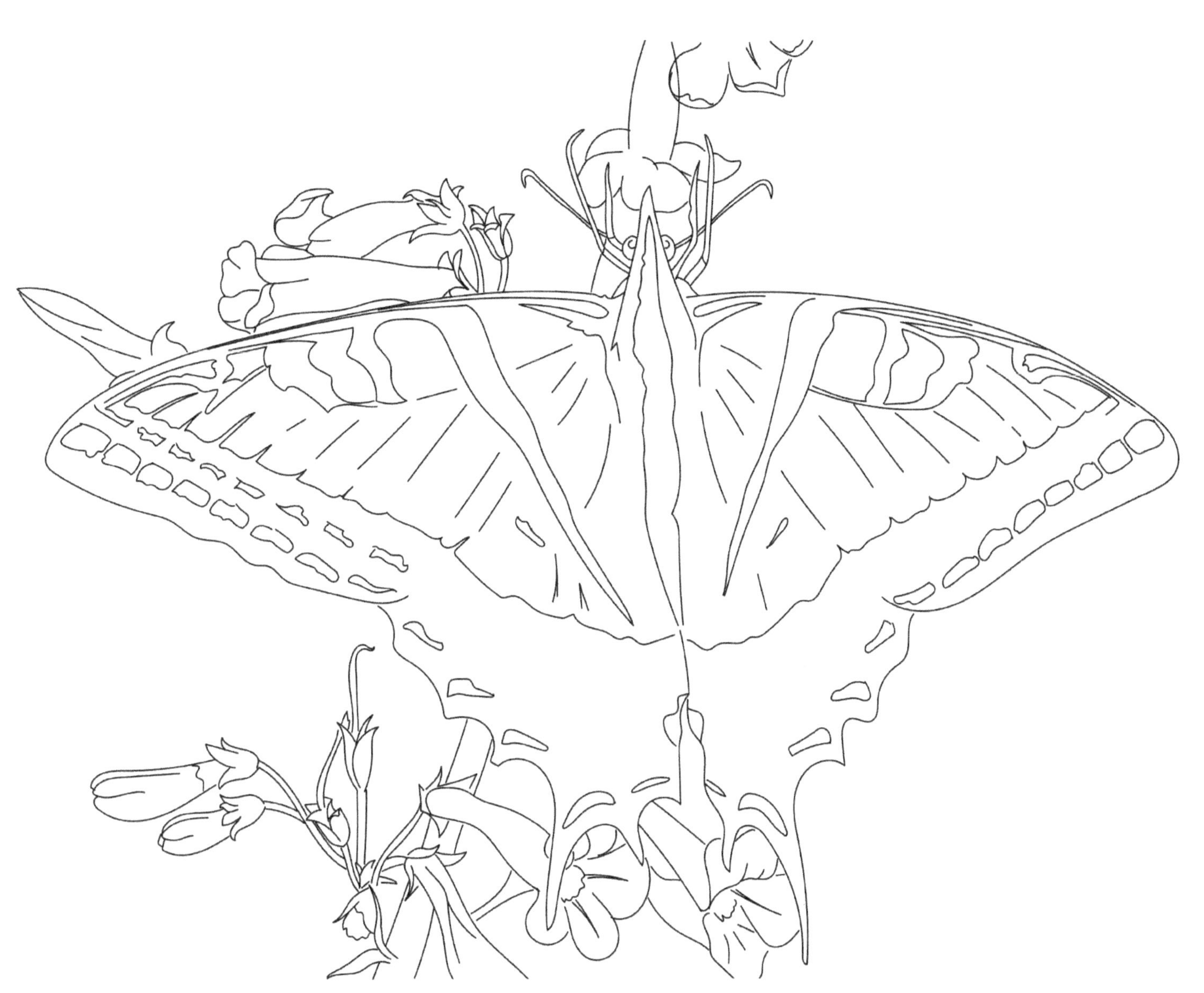

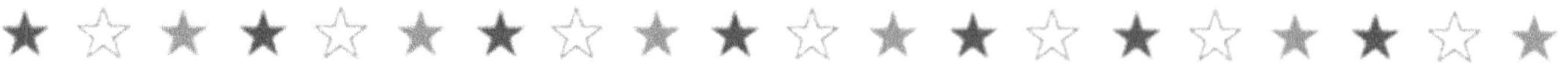

Mosquitoes in Arizona: Persistent Pests and Public Health Concerns

Mosquitoes are a significant concern in Arizona, especially during the hot summer months and monsoon season. Despite the state's dry climate, various mosquito species thrive in the region, posing both a nuisance and a public health threat due to their potential to spread diseases.

Common Mosquito Species

Aedes aegypti: Also known as the yellow fever mosquito, this species is a day-active mosquito that is an aggressive biter, particularly around dawn and dusk. It is known to transmit diseases such as yellow fever, dengue, Zika, and chikungunya.

Culex tarsalis: This species is the primary vector for West Nile virus and St. Louis encephalitis in Arizona. They are typically active during the evening and early morning hours.

Aedes vexans: Known as the inland floodwater mosquito, this species is common in Arizona and can transmit West Nile virus and dog heartworm. They are particularly aggressive biters and are most active at night.

Mosquitoes in Arizona breed in standing water, which can accumulate in natural and artificial containers such as puddles, birdbaths, flower pots, and gutters. Female mosquitoes require a blood meal to develop eggs, leading them to bite humans and animals. The presence of standing water after monsoon rains significantly increases mosquito populations.

Mosquito-borne diseases are a serious concern in Arizona. The state has experienced outbreaks of West Nile virus, with significant cases reported in Maricopa County. Other diseases transmitted by mosquitoes in the region include St. Louis encephalitis and, less commonly, dengue and malaria. Preventative measures such as eliminating standing water, using insect repellent, and installing screens on windows and doors are crucial to reducing the risk of mosquito bites and disease transmission.

Fun Facts

The mosquito lifecycle includes four stages: egg, larva, pupa, and adult. The complete cycle can take as little as one week.

Only female mosquitoes bite as they need blood for egg development. Males feed on nectar and other plant sugars.

Understanding the behavior and risks associated with mosquitoes is essential for minimizing their impact. By taking appropriate preventative measures, residents and visitors can protect themselves from mosquito bites and the diseases these insects can carry.

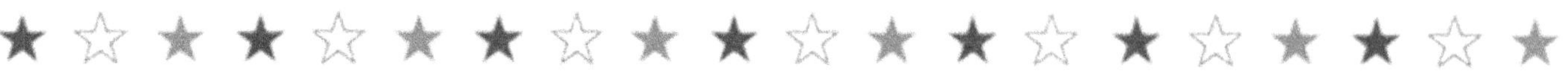

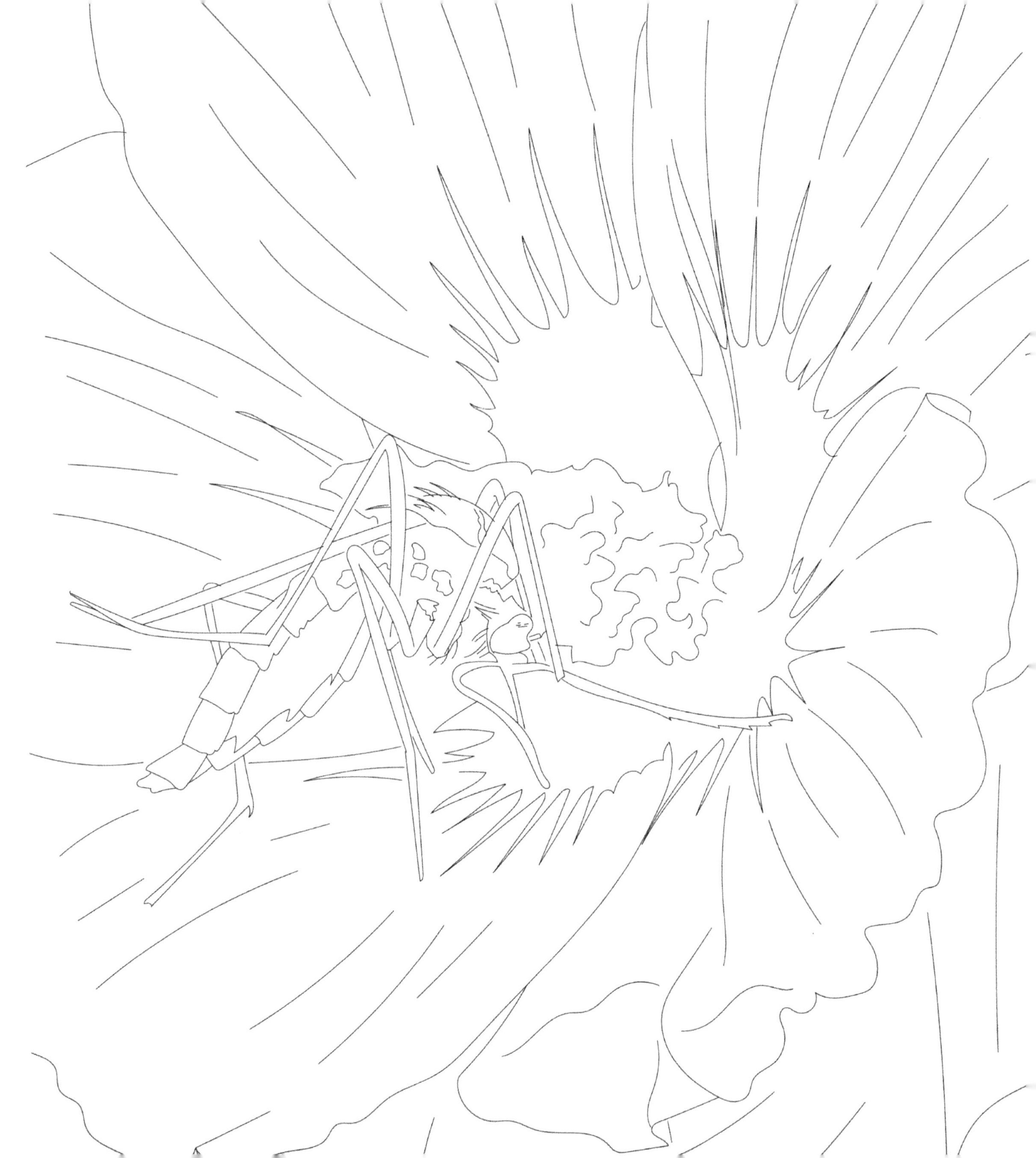

The Gila Monster

The Gila Monster (Heloderma suspectum) is one of Arizona's most iconic and fascinating reptiles. As one of only two venomous lizard species in the world (the other being its close relative, the Mexican beaded lizard), the Gila Monster holds a special place in the pantheon of Southwestern wildlife.

Named after the Gila River Basin where it was first discovered, this striking lizard can grow up to 2 feet long. Its stout body is covered in bead-like scales, creating a bumpy texture that's both visually striking and functionally protective. The Gila Monster's coloration is unmistakable - a patchwork of black with pink, orange, or yellow blotches, forming an intricate pattern that serves as a warning to potential predators.

Unlike venomous snakes that inject venom through hollow fangs, Gila Monsters have venom glands in their lower jaws. When they bite, they hang on tenaciously, chewing to work the venom into the wound. While painful, their bite is rarely fatal to humans.

Fun fact:

Gila Monster venom has led to a medical breakthrough. A compound derived from their venom, called exendin-4, has been developed into a medication to treat type 2 diabetes!

Gila Monsters are mostly active during the spring and early summer, spending up to 95% of their time underground in burrows to escape the intense desert heat. They're slow-moving and docile unless provoked, preferring to avoid confrontation.

These unique lizards have a fascinating diet, primarily feeding on eggs of ground-nesting birds and small mammals. They can eat up to one-third of their body weight in a single meal and store fat in their tails to survive long periods without food.

Protected by Arizona state law since 1952, Gila Monsters are an important part of the Sonoran Desert ecosystem. Their presence is often considered an indicator of a healthy desert environment.

Whether basking in the sun on a rocky outcrop or lumbering across the desert floor, the Gila Monster is a living testament to the diverse and extraordinary wildlife of Arizona.

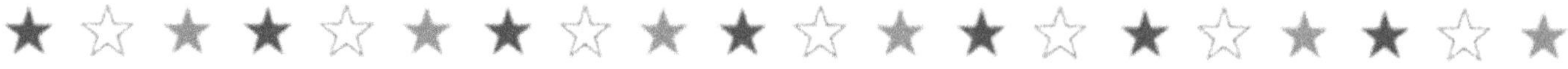

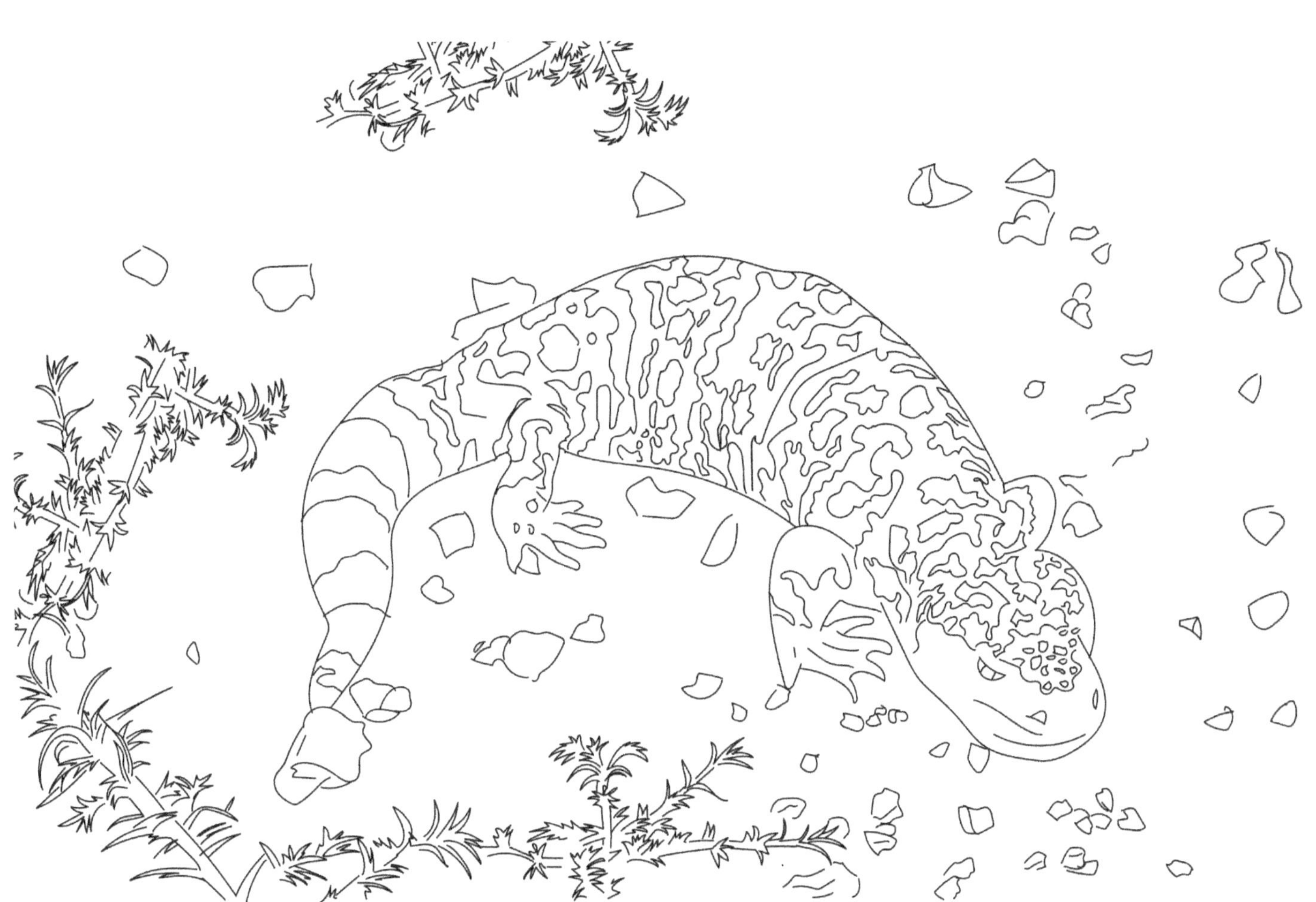

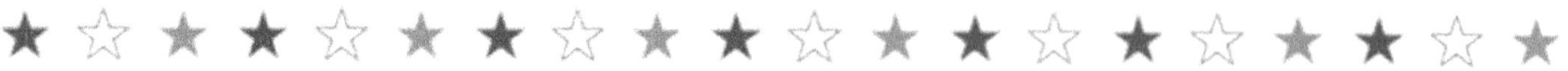

Dragonflies in Arizona: Elegant Aerial Acrobats

Dragonflies, belonging to the order Odonata, are a common and captivating sight in Arizona. These insects are known for their incredible flying abilities, vibrant colors, and important role in the ecosystem as both predators and prey.

Common Species in Arizona

Blue Dasher (Pachydiplax longipennis): Recognizable by its vibrant blue body and green eyes, the Blue Dasher is frequently seen around ponds and marshes. Males are brightly colored, while females have a more subdued brown and yellow appearance. This species is known for its territorial behavior and agile flight.

Common Green Darner (Anax junius): One of the largest and most widespread dragonflies in North America, the Common Green Darner has a bright green thorax and a blue or brown abdomen. They are strong fliers and are often seen patrolling over large bodies of water. These dragonflies are known for their long migrations, sometimes traveling hundreds of miles.

Halloween Pennant (Celithemis eponina): Named for its orange-yellow wings with dark bands, the Halloween Pennant is a striking dragonfly found near vegetated bodies of water. It is an adept flyer, capable of hunting during strong winds and rain. Unlike many dragonfly species, Halloween Pennants are not highly territorial.

Variegated Meadowhawk (Sympetrum corruptum): This species is known for its colorful appearance, with males displaying bright red, pink, or golden-brown abdomens and females being duller in color. Variegated Meadowhawks are migratory and can be seen around still or slow-moving waters, feeding on small flying insects.

Dragonflies thrive in various aquatic environments, such as ponds, lakes, marshes, and streams. They are predators both in their larval stage, where they live underwater, and as adults, where they catch flying insects like mosquitoes, flies, and moths. Their agile flight and keen vision make them efficient hunters.

Dragonflies are not only beautiful and fascinating creatures but also play a crucial role in maintaining ecological balance. Observing these aerial acrobats in their natural habitat offers a glimpse into the complexity and beauty of nature in Arizona. Whether spotting a Blue Dasher skimming over a pond or watching the territorial dance of a Common Green Darner, these insects are a testament to the vibrant biodiversity of the region.

Fun Facts

Dragonflies undergo incomplete metamorphosis, spending most of their lives as aquatic nymphs before emerging as adults. The nymph stage can last several years, while the adult stage is relatively short, usually only a few months.

As predators, dragonflies help control populations of pest insects. They are also an important food source for birds, fish, and other wildlife.

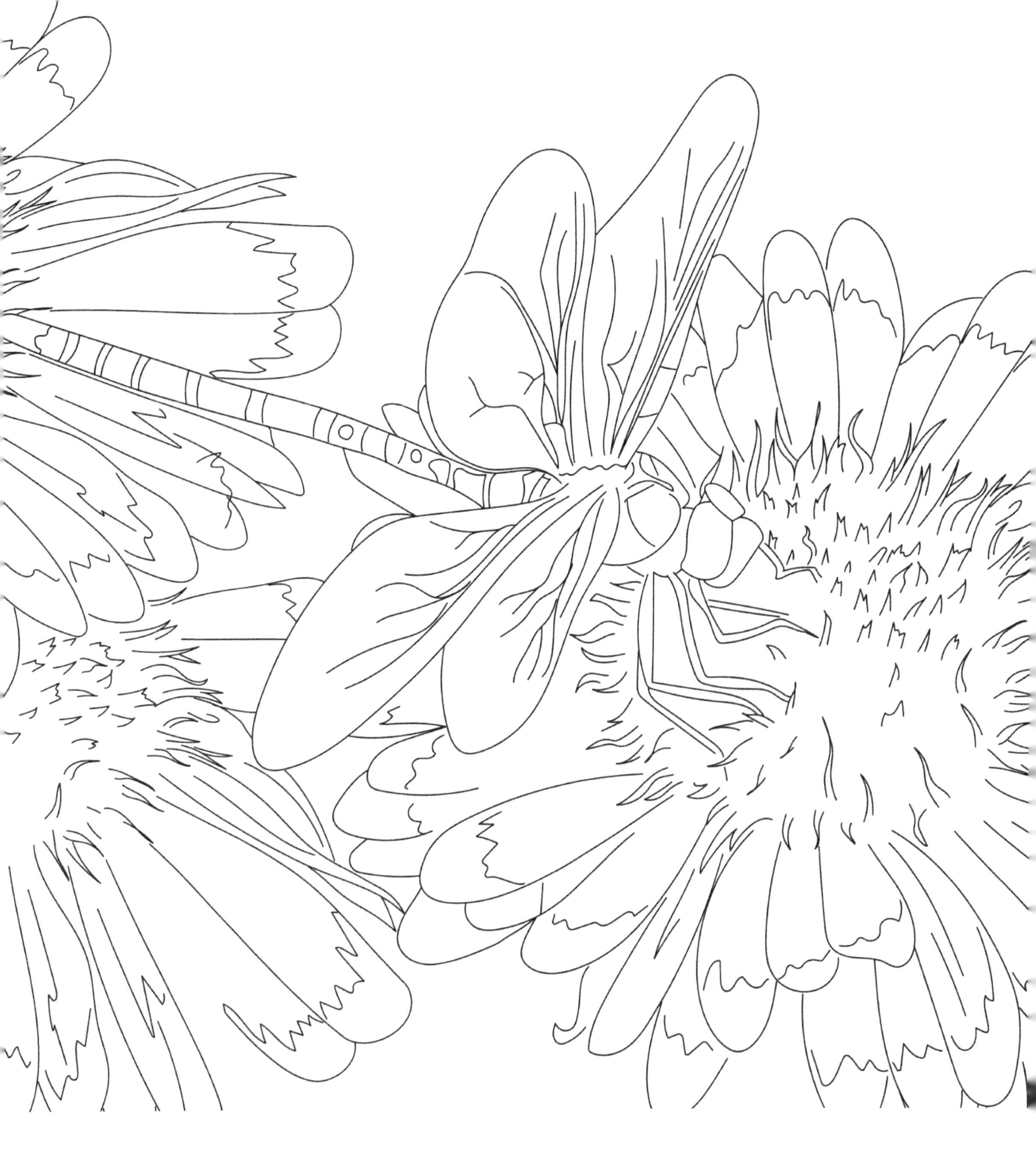

The Pigeon Horntail Wasp

The Pigeon Horntail Wasp (Tremex columba), despite its intimidating name, is a fascinating and harmless insect that plays an important role in forest ecosystems. This large, impressive wasp is actually not a true wasp at all, but belongs to a group of insects called wood wasps or horntails.

Growing up to 1.5 inches long, the Pigeon Horntail is one of the largest native wasps in North America. Females are typically larger than males and have a long, prominent ovipositor that looks like a stinger but is actually used for laying eggs. This "horn" at the tail gives the insect its common name.

The Pigeon Horntail's body is cylindrical and robust, with colors ranging from dark brown to black, often with yellow bands on the abdomen. Its wings are amber-tinted and translucent, giving it a distinctive appearance when in flight.

> *Fun fact:*
>
> Despite their fearsome look, Pigeon Horntails cannot sting! The long "stinger" on females is solely for depositing eggs into wood, not for defense.

These insects play a crucial role in forest health. Female Pigeon Horntails use their ovipositors to drill into the wood of dying or stressed hardwood trees, particularly maples and beeches, where they lay their eggs. The larvae then feed on the wood, helping to break down dead or dying trees and recycle nutrients back into the forest ecosystem.

Interestingly, the female Pigeon Horntail has a symbiotic relationship with a fungus. When laying eggs, she also deposits spores of this fungus, which helps break down the wood and provides food for her developing larvae.

While not commonly seen due to their habitat high in the forest canopy, Pigeon Horntails are an important part of woodland ecosystems across North America, including forested areas of Arizona.

The Pigeon Horntail Wasp, with its unique appearance and fascinating life cycle, represents the intricate and often overlooked relationships that maintain the health of our forests.

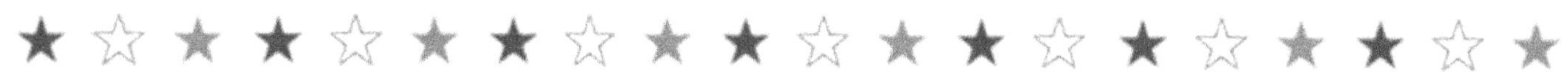

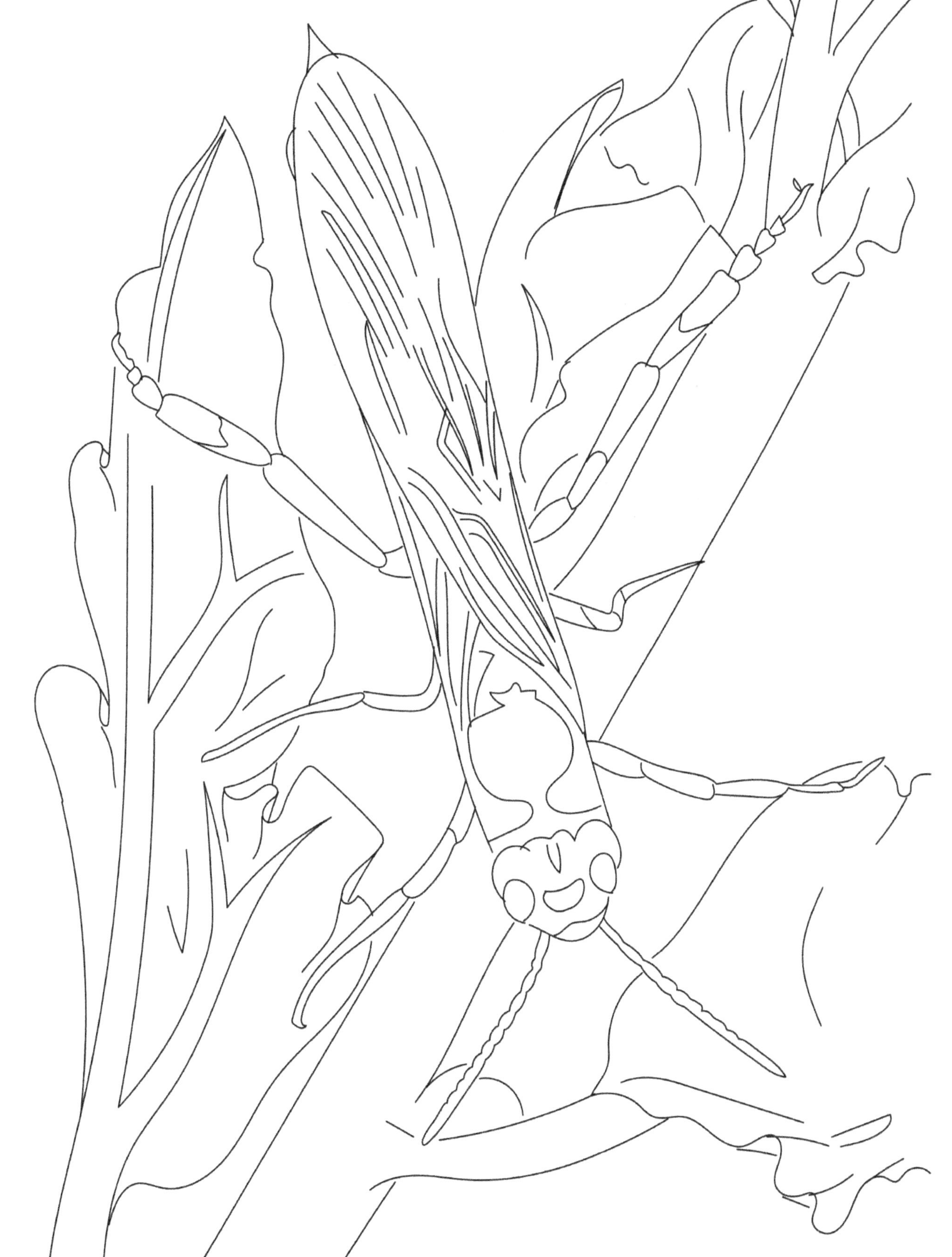

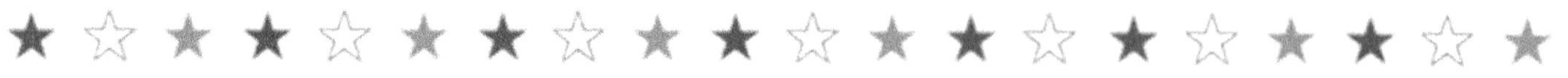

The Arizona Bee: Nature's Busy Desert Pollinators

Arizona is home to a diverse array of bee species, each playing a crucial role in the state's unique ecosystem. From the iconic honeybee to native species like the Sonoran bumble bee, these industrious insects are essential to the health and beauty of Arizona's landscapes.

One of the most fascinating native bees is the Sonoran Carpenter Bee. These large, striking bees are often mistaken for bumblebees due to their size. However, they're distinguished by their shiny, black bodies and their habit of nesting in wood rather than in the ground.

Bees in Arizona have adapted to the harsh desert environment in remarkable ways. Many species are active in the early morning or late evening to avoid the intense midday heat. Some have even developed special "hair" on their bodies to help collect and distribute water, a precious resource in the desert.

> ### *Fun fact:*
>
> **Arizona is home to the rare Cochise Bumble Bee, found only in the sky islands of southeastern Arizona and parts of Mexico. This species is specially adapted to high-altitude environments!**

Bees are vital pollinators for many of Arizona's iconic plants. From the towering saguaro cactus to delicate wildflowers, these plants rely on bees for reproduction. In turn, the unique flora of Arizona provides a diverse buffet of nectar and pollen for the bees.

Urban areas in Arizona are increasingly recognizing the importance of bees. Many cities, including Payson, are encouraging bee-friendly gardening practices and the creation of pollinator habitats in parks and public spaces.

Whether you spot them buzzing around a flowering cactus or pollinating a backyard garden, Arizona's bees are fascinating creatures that play a crucial role in maintaining the state's biodiversity. Their presence is a reminder of the intricate connections within nature and the importance of preserving our natural environments.

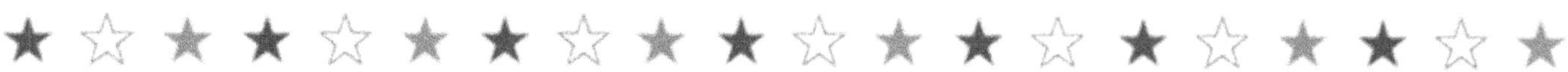

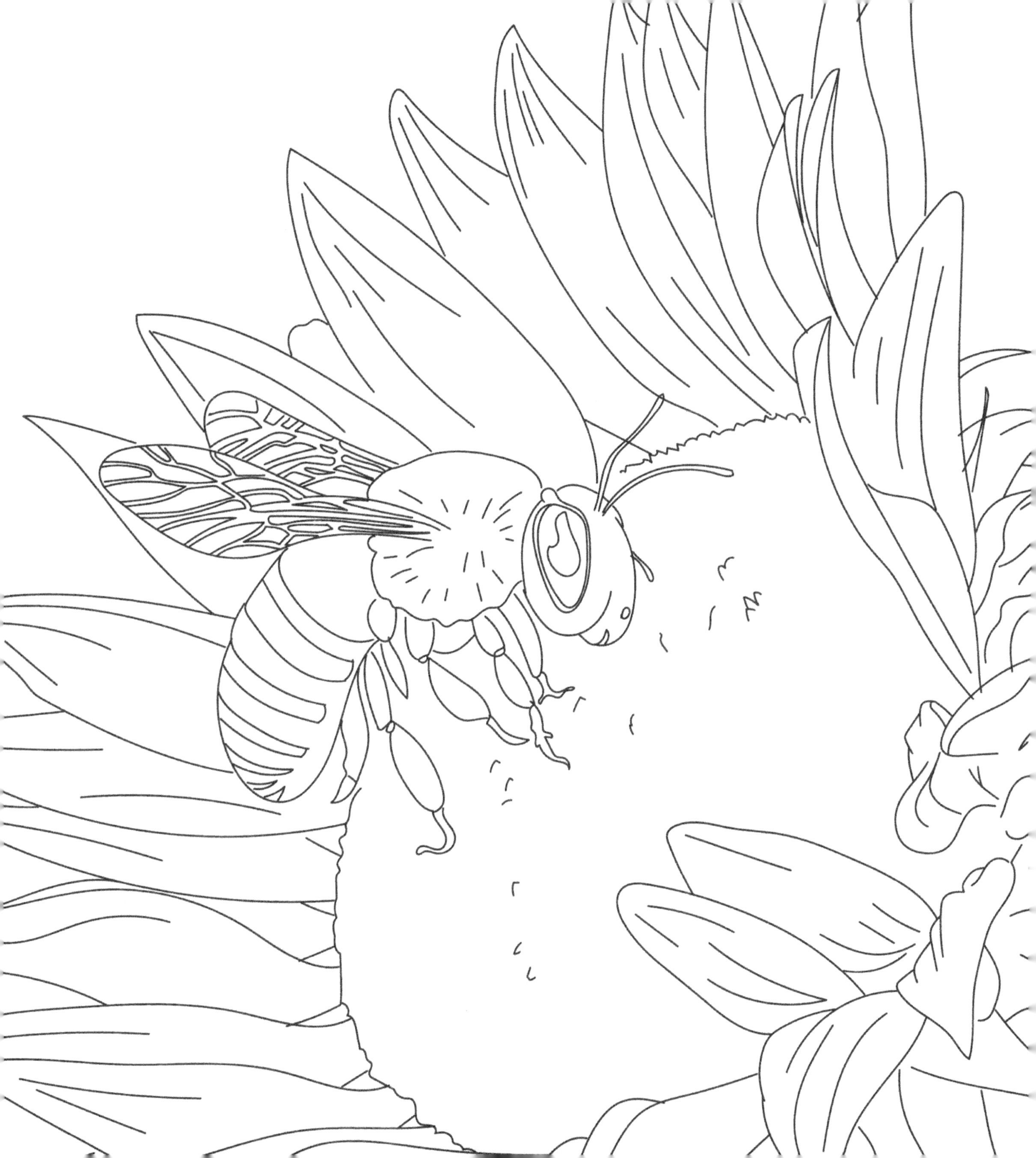

The Horned Toad Lizard

The horned toad lizard, despite its name, is not actually a toad but a lizard of the genus Phrynosoma. These unique creatures are found in various habitats across Arizona, from desert floors to grasslands. Their flat, round bodies and crown of horns give them a distinctive, almost prehistoric appearance that has captivated people for generations.

Horned lizards are masters of camouflage, their bodies typically colored in shades of tan, gray, or reddish-brown to match the soil and rocks of their environment. Their rough, spiky skin texture further helps them blend into their surroundings. The most prominent feature is the crown of horns on their head, which varies in size and number depending on the species.

These lizards have a unique diet, specializing in eating ants. Their bodies are specially adapted to digest these insects, which most other animals avoid due to their acidic nature. Horned lizards can consume thousands of ants in a single day!

In Arizona, the most common species is the Greater Short-horned Lizard, also known as the Mountain Short-horned Lizard. These creatures play an important role in their ecosystem, helping to control ant populations and serving as prey for various birds and mammals.

Unfortunately, horned lizard populations have declined in some areas due to habitat loss and the introduction of non-native ant species. Conservation efforts are ongoing to protect these unique reptiles.

Whether basking in the sun on a rock or scurrying across the desert floor, horned toad lizards are a fascinating example of Arizona's diverse and adaptable wildlife. Their intricate patterns and unusual form make them an excellent subject for detailed coloring projects, allowing artists to explore the unique textures and features of these remarkable creatures.

> ### *Fun fact:*
>
> When threatened, some species of horned lizards have an extraordinary defense mechanism - they can squirt blood from their eyes! This startling behavior, which can project blood up to 5 feet, is used to confuse predators and give the lizard a chance to escape.

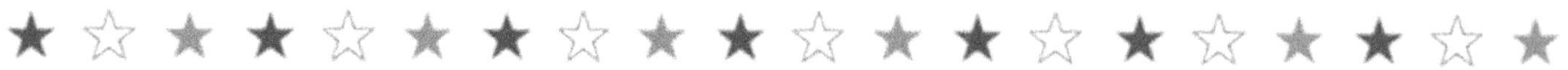

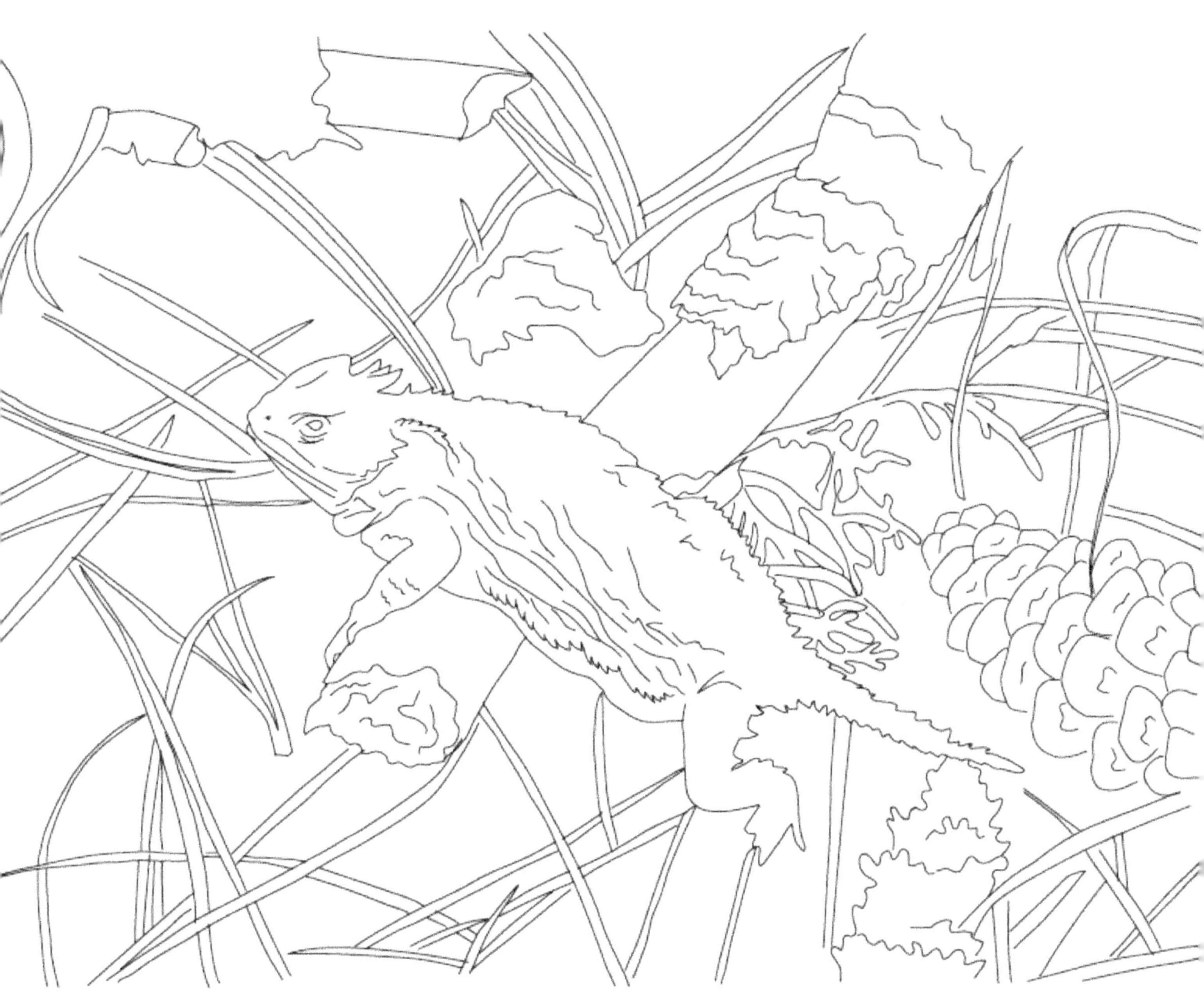

Arizona Snakes

Arizona is home to a diverse array of snake species, including some colorful and distinctive varieties as shown in these drwaings .

The first image shows a California Kingsnake, known for its striking pattern of alternating black and white or reddish-orange bands. These non-venomous snakes are constrictors and are famous for their ability to eat other snakes, including rattlesnakes.

The second drawing depicts a Western Diamondback Rattlesnake, one of Arizona's most well-known venomous snakes. It has a thick body with diamond-shaped patterns along its back and a distinctive rattle at the end of its tail. When threatened, it coils and rattles as a warning before striking.

Fun fact:

The Sonoran Coral Snake, another Arizona native (not pictured), has a venomous bite but a mouth too small to effectively bite humans. It's known for the rhyme "Red touch yellow, kill a fellow; red touch black, venom lack" which helps distinguish it from similar-looking non-venomous snakes.

The third drawing shows a Gopher Snake, also known as a Bull Snake. These large, non-venomous snakes are often mistaken for rattlesnakes due to their similar coloration and defensive behavior. When threatened, they may flatten their heads, hiss loudly, and vibrate their tails to mimic a rattlesnake.

Arizona's snake population plays a crucial role in controlling rodent populations and maintaining the balance of desert ecosystems. While some species are venomous, most snakes in Arizona are harmless to humans and prefer to avoid confrontation.

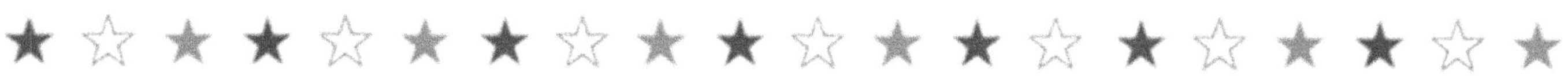

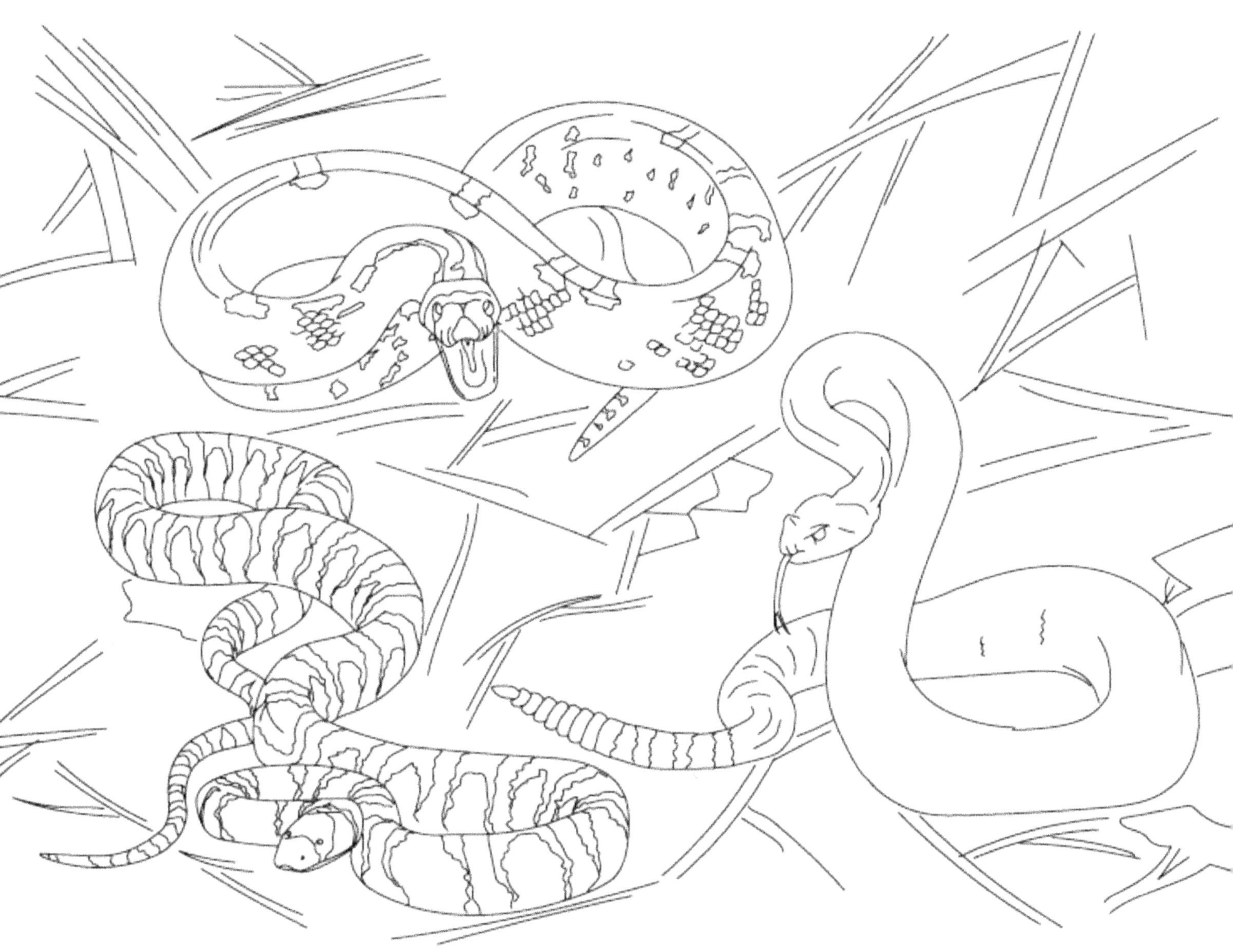

The Arizona Butterfly

Arizona's diverse landscapes are a haven for a stunning variety of butterflies, with over 300 species fluttering through the state's deserts, mountains, and canyons. These delicate insects add bursts of color and movement to Arizona's natural tapestry.

One of the most iconic is the Two-tailed Swallowtail, Arizona's state butterfly. With its large size and distinctive yellow and black pattern adorned with blue crescents and red spots, it's a true showstopper. These beautiful creatures can often be seen gracefully floating through Arizona's pine forests and canyons.

The Monarch butterfly, known for its incredible multi-generation migration, also passes through Arizona. These orange and black beauties use the state as a pit stop on their long journey between Mexico and Canada.

For a touch of local flair, the Arizona Sister butterfly is a sight to behold. Its dark wings with white bands and orange spots near the tips make it stand out as it flits through oak and pine woodlands in the state's sky islands.

Fun fact:

The Pipevine Swallowtail has a unique defense mechanism. As a caterpillar, it feeds on pipevine plants, which are toxic to most animals. The butterfly retains these toxins into adulthood, making it unpalatable to predators. Its striking blue-black wings with iridescent blue hindwings serve as a warning of its toxicity.

Arizona's butterflies play crucial roles in their ecosystems as pollinators and food sources for other wildlife. From the tiny Western Pygmy Blue, one of the world's smallest butterflies, to the large and showy Queen butterfly, these insects are not just beautiful but also essential components of Arizona's biodiversity.

Whether you spot them in a Sonoran Desert botanical garden or high in the Mogollon Rim's meadows, Arizona's butterflies offer a enchanting display of nature's artistry, delighting observers with their colors, patterns, and graceful flight.

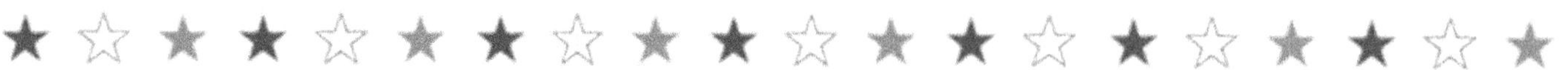

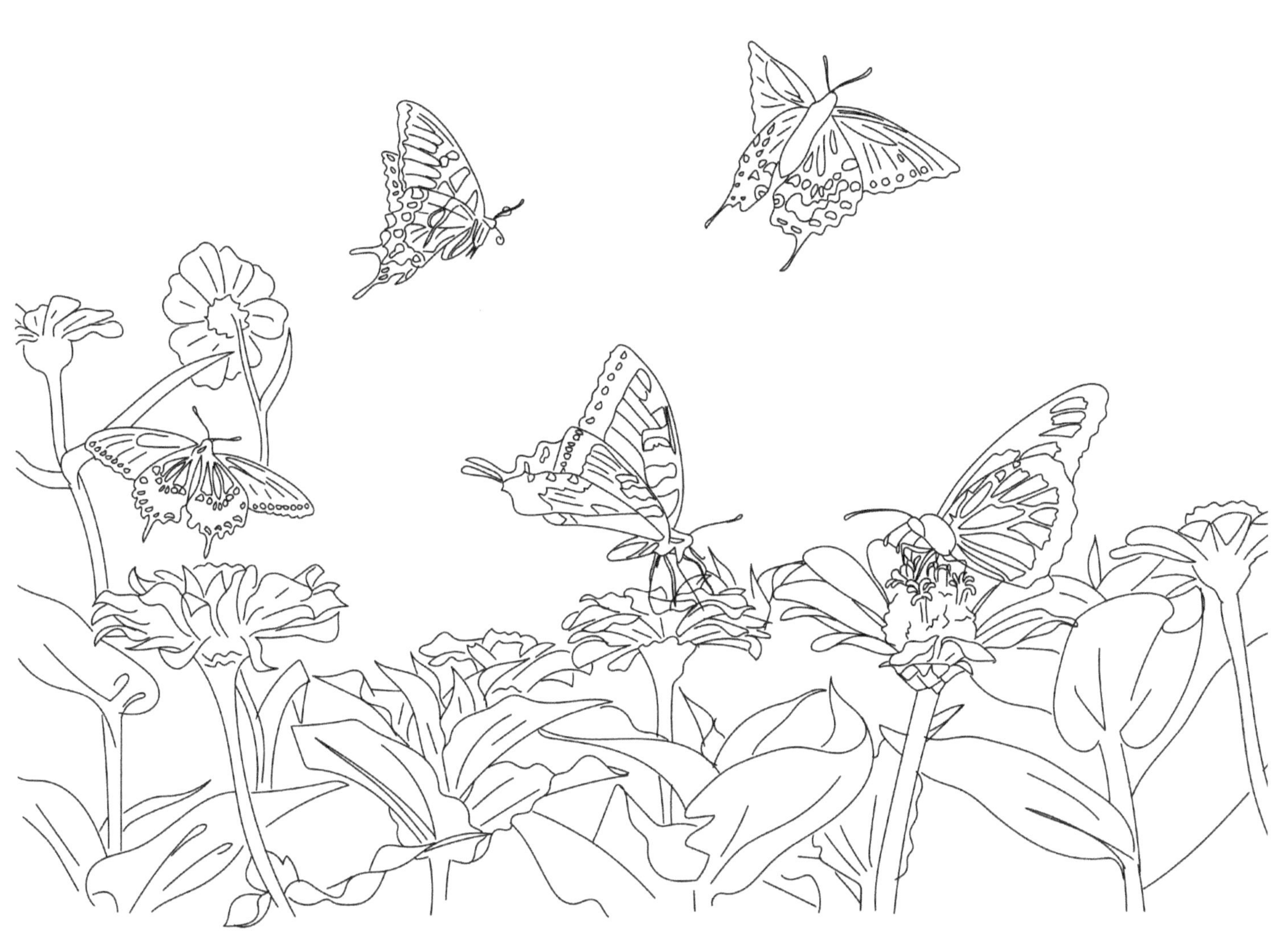

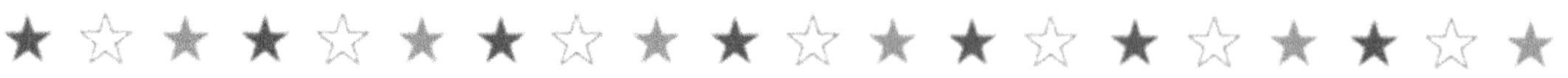

The Arizona Wren

The Arizona Wren, or Cactus Wren (Campylorhynchus brunneicapillus), is a charismatic desert dweller. About 7-9 inches long, it sports a speckled brown and white plumage, perfect for blending into its arid habitat. Its long, slightly curved beak is ideal for probing cacti and shrubs for insects.

These wrens are known for their loud, raspy calls that echo across the desert landscape. They're often seen in pairs, as they mate for life. Arizona Wrens are resourceful birds, making their nests in cholla cacti, yucca plants, or even in the crooks of saguaro arms.

Fun fact:

Arizona Wrens are talented architects! They build intricate, football-shaped nests with small entrance tubes. These nests are so well-constructed that they can last for years, often being reused by subsequent generations of wrens. The multiple decoy nests they build aren't just for predator confusion – they also use them as "guest rooms" for roosting on cold nights.

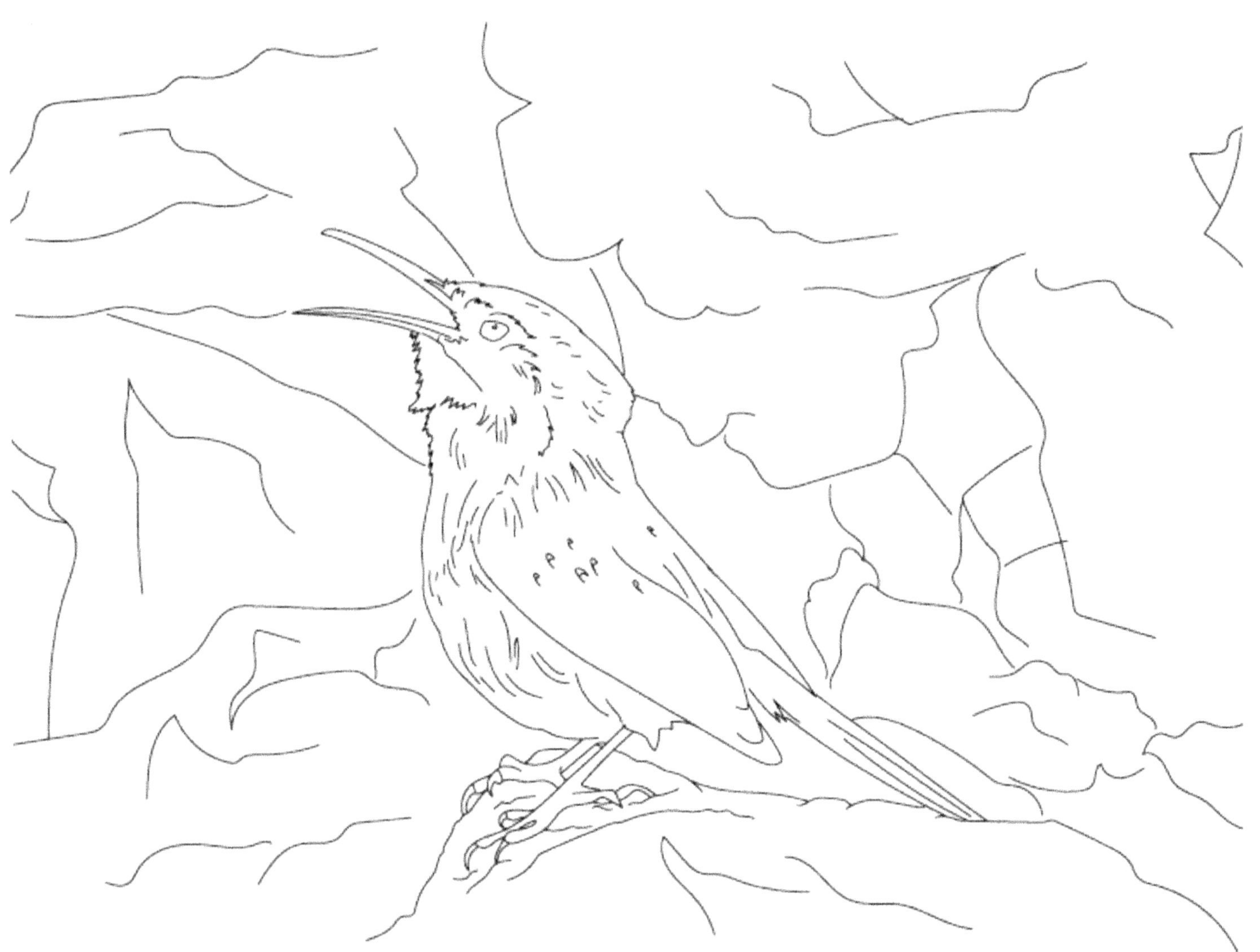

Red-tailed Hawk

The Red-tailed Hawk (Buteo jamaicensis) is one of North America's most widespread and recognizable birds of prey. These majestic raptors are a common sight in Arizona's skies, from desert lowlands to high mountain forests.

Known for their imposing size and distinctive rusty-red tail, adult Red-tailed Hawks typically have a dark brown back and a pale underside with a streaked belly. Their broad, rounded wings and short, wide tail give them a characteristic silhouette when soaring. With a wingspan that can reach up to 4.5 feet, they cut an impressive figure against the azure Arizona sky.

These hawks are supremely adapted predators. Their sharp, hooked beaks and powerful talons are perfect for catching and consuming prey, which typically includes small mammals, birds, and reptiles. Their keen eyesight is about eight times sharper than a human's, allowing them to spot potential meals from great heights.

In Arizona, Red-tailed Hawks can be found year-round. They're often seen perched on tall trees, telephone poles, or soaring in wide circles high above open fields, using rising thermal air currents to stay aloft with minimal effort.

Fun fact:

The Red-tailed Hawk's scream is one of the most familiar bird sounds in North America, often used in movies and TV shows as a generic bird of prey call, even for eagles!

During breeding season, pairs of Red-tailed Hawks perform spectacular courtship displays, soaring in wide circles and occasionally locking talons in mid-air. They build large stick nests high in trees or on cliff ledges, often reusing and adding to the same nest year after year.

The Red-tailed Hawk plays a crucial role in maintaining ecological balance by helping to control populations of small mammals. Their presence in an area is often an indicator of a healthy ecosystem.

Whether you spot one perched regally on a saguaro cactus or circling high above Arizona's varied landscapes, the Red-tailed Hawk embodies the wild spirit and adaptability of the American Southwest.

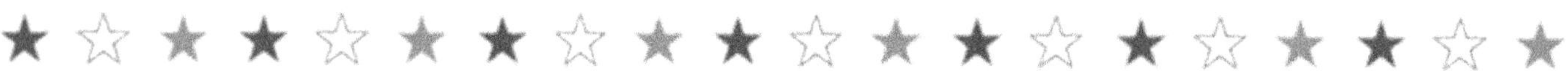

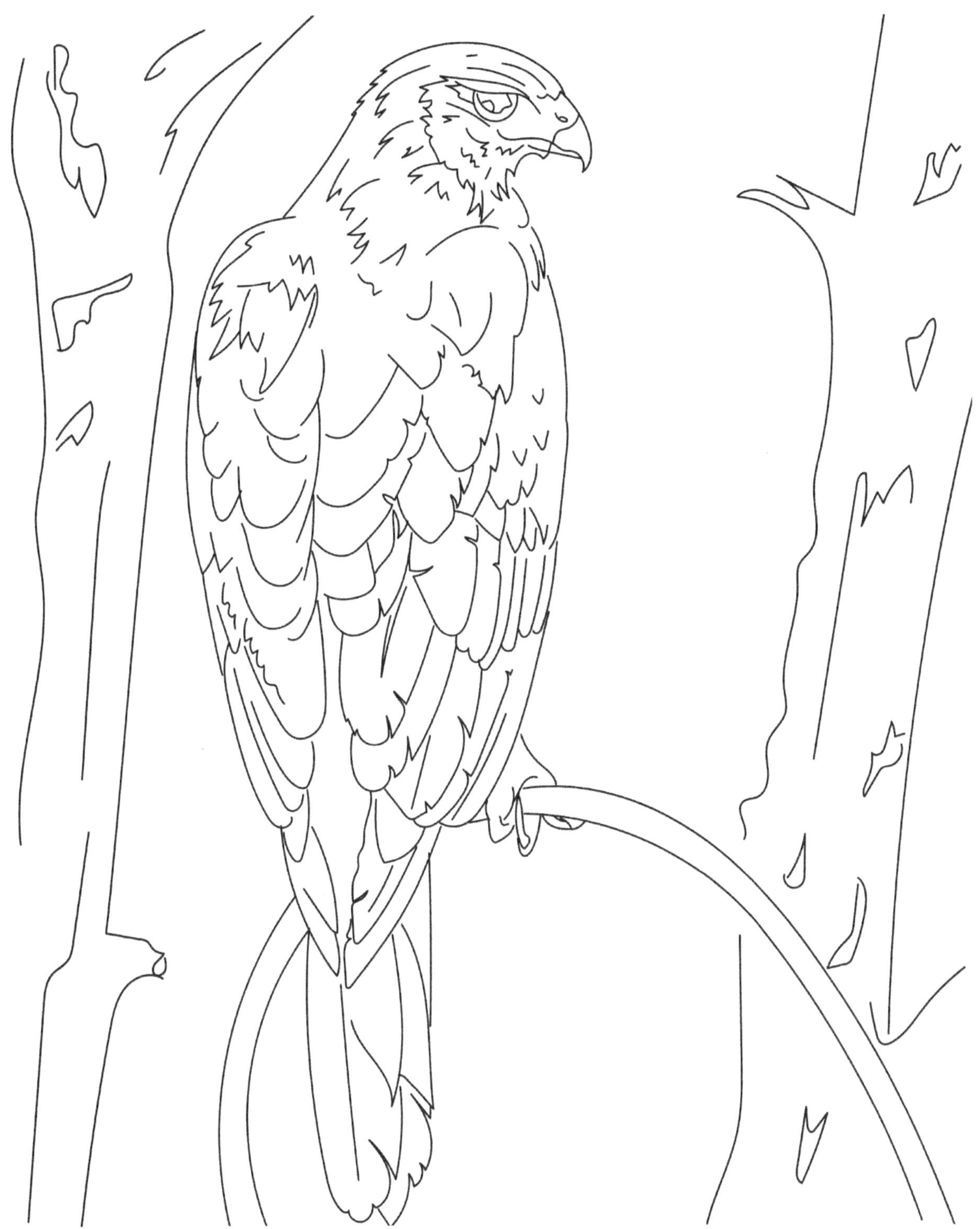

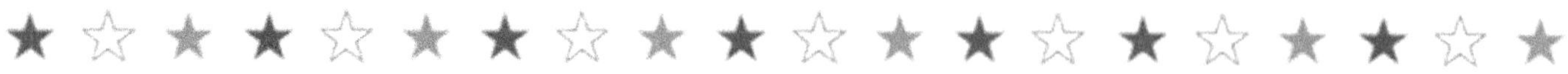

The Arizona Woodpecker

The Arizona Woodpecker (Leuconotopicus arizonae) is a unique and charming bird native to the southwestern United States, including its namesake state of Arizona. This medium-sized woodpecker is a true gem of the region's pine-oak forests and mountain canyons.

Unlike many of its flashier woodpecker cousins, the Arizona Woodpecker sports a more subdued but elegant appearance. Its back is a rich brown color, contrasting nicely with its white-spotted wings and tail. Males can be distinguished by their bright red cap, while females have an all-brown head.

Standing about 7-8 inches tall, these industrious birds can often be seen clinging to tree trunks and branches, using their strong beaks to probe for insects hidden beneath the bark. Their distinctive drumming echoes through the wooded canyons, a rhythmic soundtrack to Arizona's high-country forests.

Fun fact:

The Arizona Woodpecker is the only brown-backed woodpecker found in the United States! This makes it a special find for birdwatchers and nature enthusiasts exploring Arizona's diverse avian population.

These woodpeckers play a crucial role in their ecosystem. As they search for food, they create small holes in trees that later serve as nesting sites for other cavity-nesting birds. They also help control insect populations, particularly wood-boring beetles that can damage trees.

The Arizona Woodpecker's range is quite limited within the U.S., making it a true specialty of the region. Its presence in the sky islands and mountain forests of southeastern Arizona offers a unique glimpse into the state's rich biodiversity and the special creatures that call this rugged landscape home.

Whether you're hiking through Madera Canyon or exploring the Chiricahua Mountains, keep an eye (and an ear) out for this charismatic Arizona native – a living symbol of the state's wild and wonderful natural heritage.

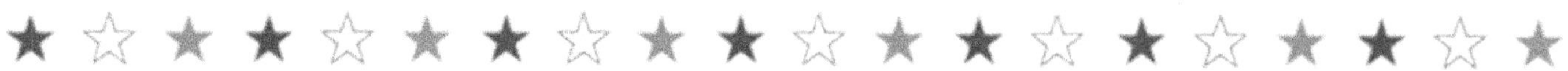

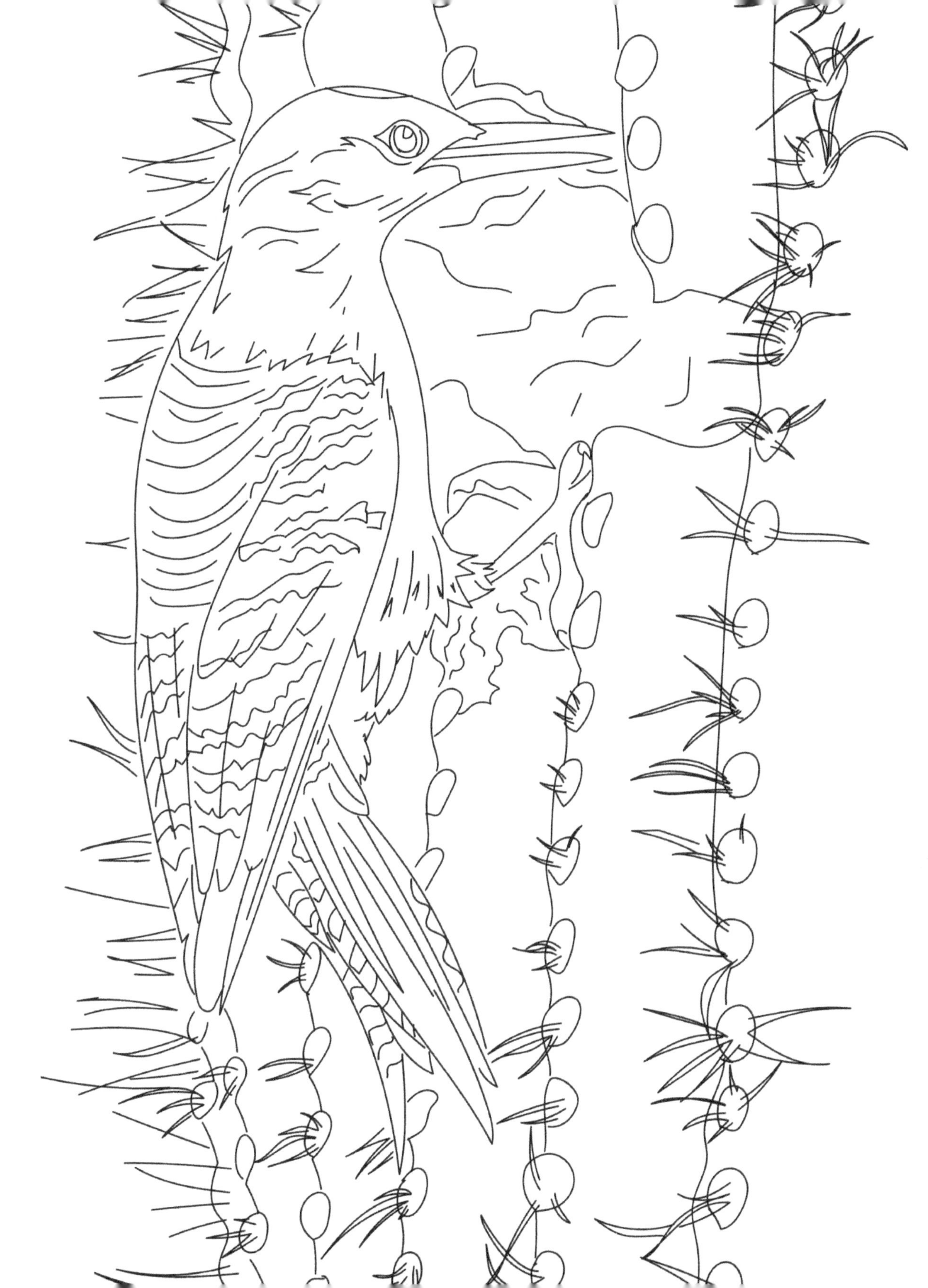

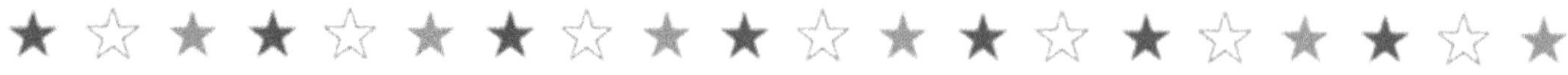

The Arizona Hummingbird

Arizona is a hummingbird haven, boasting an impressive variety of these tiny, vibrant birds. With 18 species recorded in the state, Arizona offers some of the best hummingbird watching in the United States.

One of the most common is the Anna's Hummingbird, a year-round resident known for its iridescent emerald feathers and rose-pink throat patch in males. These feisty little birds are often seen zipping around gardens and feeders throughout Arizona.

The Broad-billed Hummingbird, with its brilliant blue-green body and bright red bill, is a dazzling sight in southern Arizona. These jewel-like birds are most common in the state's sky islands and canyon areas.

For a truly special treat, look for the Magnificent Hummingbird in Arizona's mountainous regions. As its name suggests, this species is one of the largest hummingbirds in North America, with males sporting a purple crown and emerald green throat.

Fun fact:

Hummingbirds have incredible flying abilities. They can hover, fly backwards, and even upside down! Their wings beat so fast – up to 80 times per second – that they make a humming sound, which gives these birds their name.

Arizona's diverse landscapes provide crucial habitats for both resident and migratory hummingbird species. From the Sonoran Desert's cactus blooms to the nectar-rich flowers of high-altitude meadows, these tiny birds find food and shelter across the state's varied ecosystems.

Hummingbirds play a vital role as pollinators, helping to maintain the health and diversity of Arizona's plant life. Their long beaks and ability to hover make them perfectly adapted for sipping nectar from tubular flowers, many of which rely on hummingbirds for pollination.

Whether you're watching them battle for territory at a feeder or admiring their acrobatic flights among wildflowers, Arizona's hummingbirds offer endless fascination and beauty, embodying the vibrant spirit of the state's natural wonders.

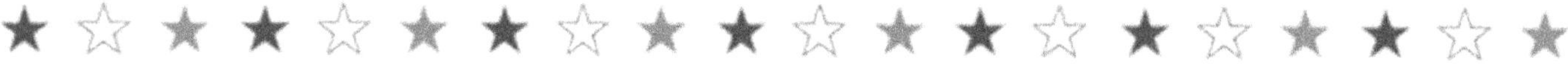

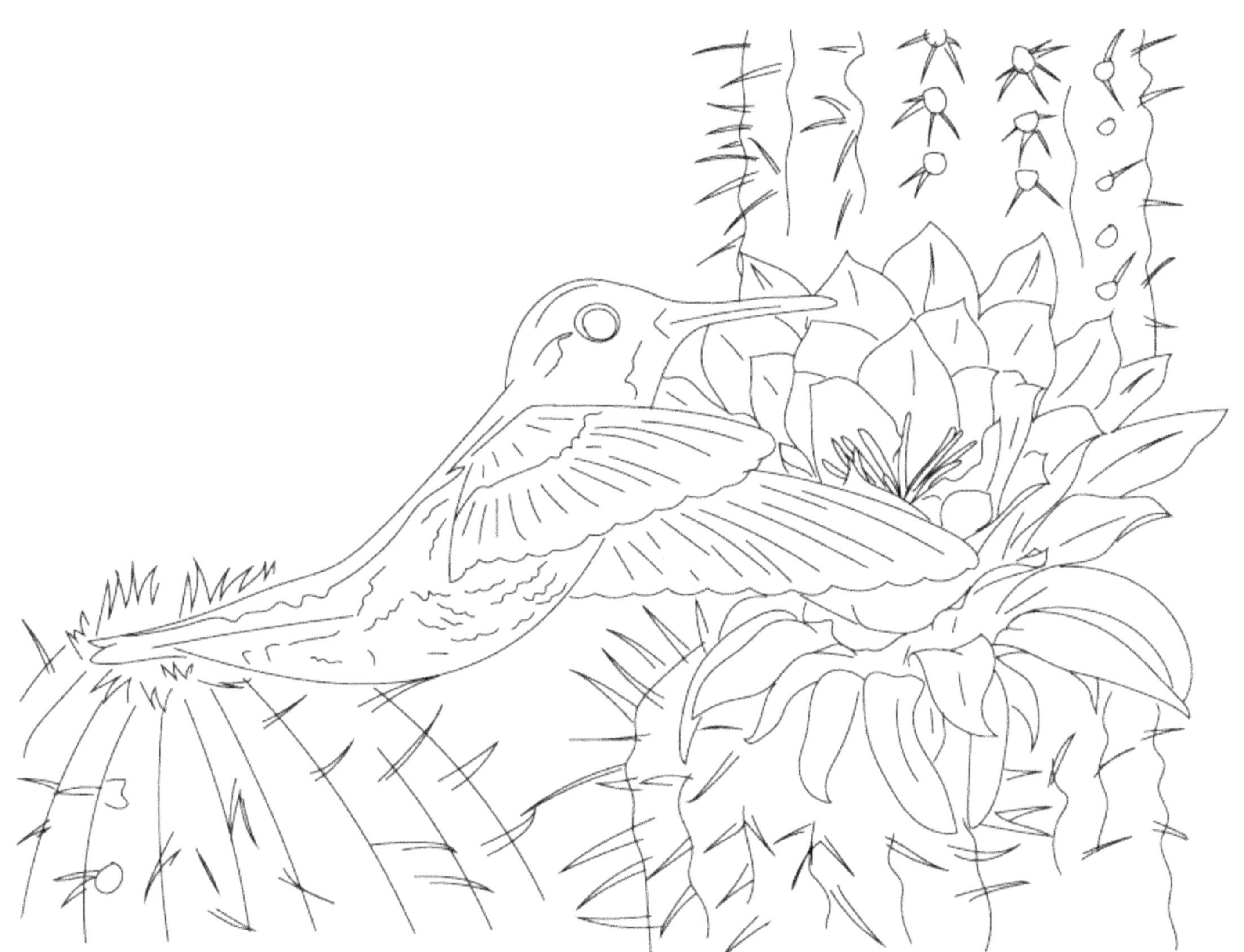

The American Bald Eagle

The American Bald Eagle (Haliaeetus leucocephalus) is one of North America's most iconic and majestic birds. Despite its name, the bald eagle isn't actually bald; its head is covered with white feathers that contrast sharply with its dark brown body and wings, giving it a distinctive and regal appearance.

These impressive birds of prey have a wingspan that can reach up to 7.5 feet, making them one of the largest birds in North America. Their powerful yellow beaks are hooked for tearing prey, and their talons are razor-sharp for catching fish, their preferred food.

Bald eagles are known for their keen eyesight, which is estimated to be four to eight times sharper than that of humans. This exceptional vision helps them spot fish from great heights as they soar above lakes and rivers.

> ### *Fun fact:*
>
> The bald eagle's distinctive white head and tail feathers don't appear until the bird is about five years old. Young eagles are mostly dark brown with occasional white mottling.

As a symbol of the United States since 1782, the bald eagle represents strength, freedom, and independence. Their comeback from the brink of extinction in the mid-20th century due to DDT poisoning is one of America's greatest conservation success stories.

In Arizona, bald eagles can be spotted near lakes and rivers, including Woods Canyon Lake, where they nest and hunt. During winter, more eagles migrate to the state, increasing the chances of sighting these magnificent birds.

Bald eagles build enormous nests, often in tall trees near water. These nests are among the largest of any bird in North America, sometimes weighing up to a ton and measuring up to 8 feet wide.

Whether soaring high in the sky, perched regally on a tree branch, or diving for fish with incredible precision, the American Bald Eagle is a breathtaking sight that embodies the wild beauty of North American wildlife.

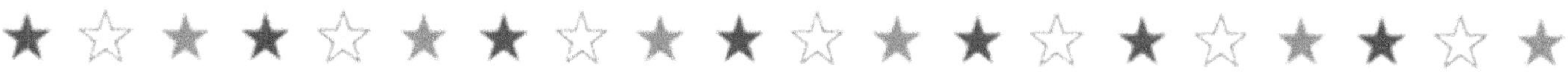

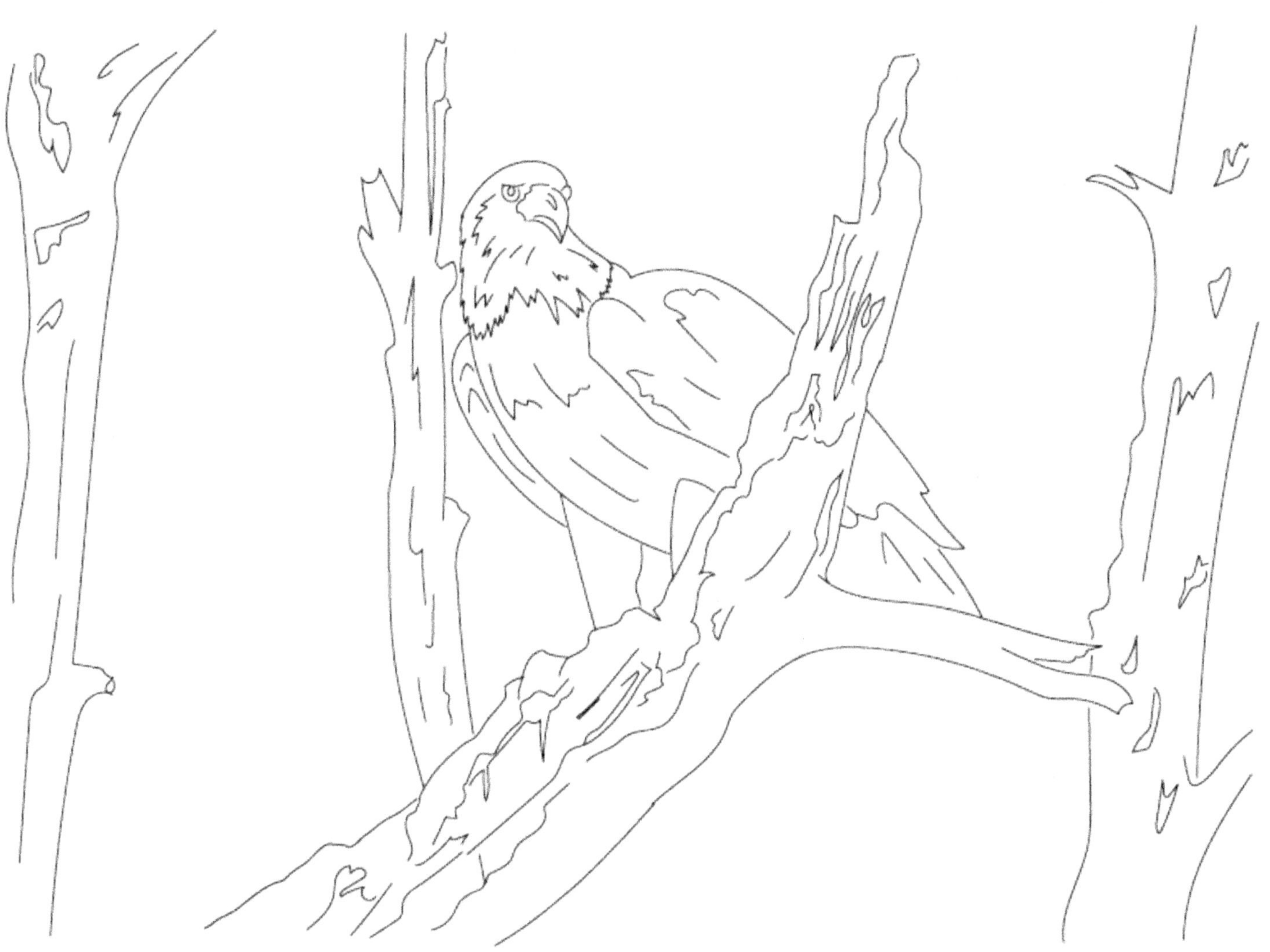

The Arizona Turkey Vulture: Nature's Clean-Up Crew

Soaring high above the diverse landscapes of Arizona, from the Sonoran Desert to the pine-covered mountains near Payson, the Turkey Vulture is a common yet fascinating sight. With its distinctive red head and broad, V-shaped wings, this large bird is an important part of Arizona's ecosystem.

Despite their somewhat intimidating appearance, Turkey Vultures are gentle creatures that play a crucial role in nature. These birds are nature's clean-up crew, feeding primarily on carrion (dead animals). This important job helps prevent the spread of disease and recycles nutrients back into the ecosystem.

Turkey Vultures are masters of the air, often seen riding thermal currents with barely a flap of their wings. They can soar for hours, using their keen sense of smell to locate their next meal. Unlike most birds, Turkey Vultures have an excellent sense of smell, which helps them find food even when it's hidden from view.

Fun fact:

When threatened, Turkey Vultures have a unique defense mechanism - they can projectile vomit! This not only startles predators but also lightens their body weight for a quicker escape.

In Arizona, Turkey Vultures are migratory. They arrive in the spring to breed and raise their young, often nesting in caves, hollow trees, or dense thickets. Come fall, most will head south for warmer climates, though some may stay year-round in the southern parts of the state.

While they may not win any beauty contests, Turkey Vultures are remarkably clean birds. They bathe frequently and spend a lot of time preening their feathers. Their bare heads, while perhaps not aesthetically pleasing to some, serve an important purpose - it helps keep them clean when feeding on messy carcasses.

Whether you spot them circling high overhead or perched with wings spread to catch the morning sun, Turkey Vultures are a reminder of nature's efficiency and the important role every creature plays in the balance of life.

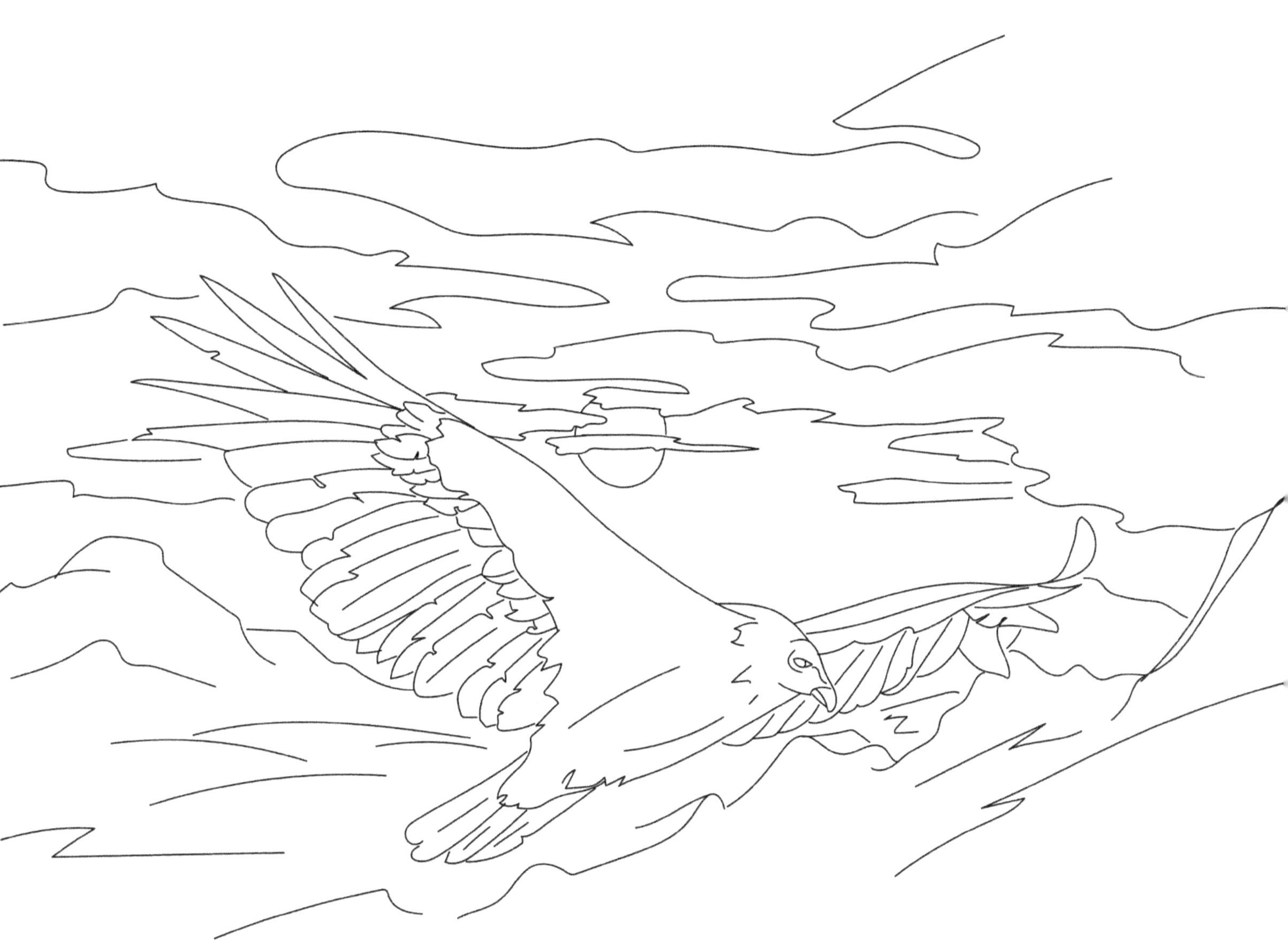

Robinia neomexicana: The New Mexico Locust

Robinia neomexicana, commonly known as the New Mexico Locust or Desert Locust, is a fascinating native tree that graces the landscapes of Payson and much of Arizona's high country. Despite its name, this hardy plant is not limited to New Mexico but thrives throughout the American Southwest.

This small tree or large shrub is a member of the pea family, related to the more widely known Black Locust. It typically grows to heights of 10-25 feet, forming thickets with its spreading roots. The New Mexico Locust is known for its beautiful, fragrant flowers that bloom in late spring to early summer.

The flowers of Robinia neomexicana are a sight to behold. They appear in showy clusters of pink to purple blossoms, each cluster containing 5-15 flowers. These sweet-scented blooms not only add beauty to the landscape but also attract a variety of pollinators, including bees and hummingbirds.

Beyond its aesthetic value, this tree plays important ecological roles. Its roots help stabilize soil, making it valuable for erosion control. As a legume, it can fix nitrogen in the soil, improving soil fertility for other plants.

Fun fact:

The New Mexico Locust has sharp thorns along its branches, an adaptation that helps protect it from browsing animals in its arid native habitat.

The New Mexico Locust is well-adapted to Payson's climate, thriving in full sun and tolerating drought once established. Its ability to withstand harsh conditions makes it a valuable plant in natural areas and in landscaping.

Native Americans have traditionally used various parts of the tree for medicinal purposes and for crafting tools. The hard, durable wood has been used for fence posts and tool handles.

Whether you spot it along a hiking trail or in a local park, the New Mexico Locust stands as a beautiful example of the diverse and resilient flora that calls Payson and the Arizona highlands home.

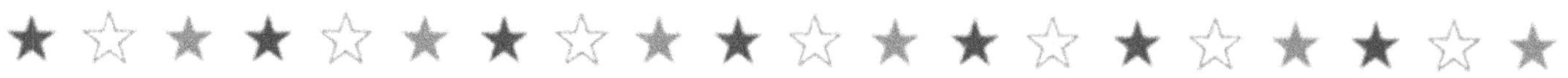

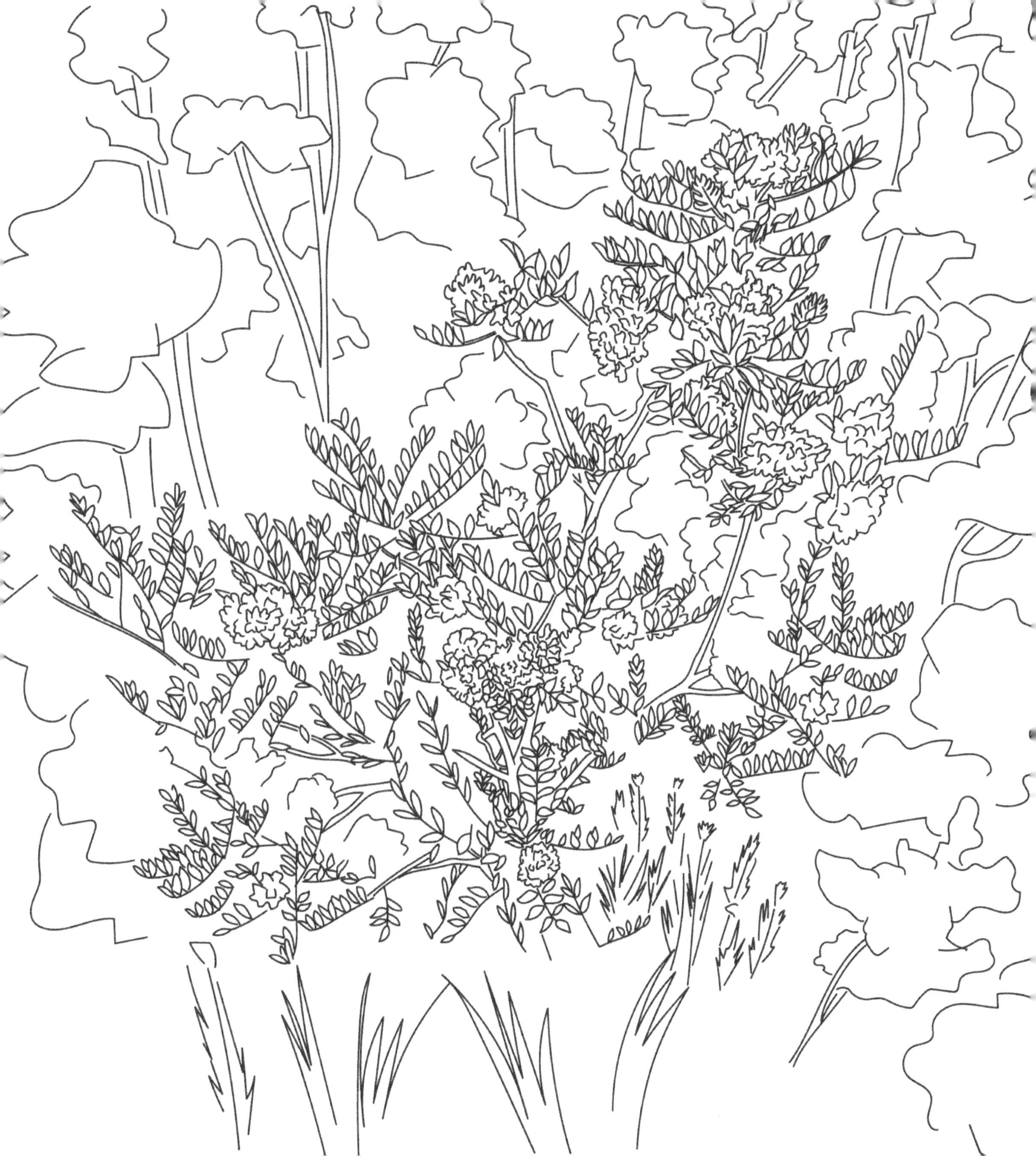

The Strawberry Schoolhouse

The Strawberry Schoolhouse: A Piece of Arizona's Educational Heritage

Nestled in the picturesque community of Strawberry, just north of Pine and about 20 minutes from Payson, stands a charming piece of Arizona's history - the Strawberry Schoolhouse. This one-room schoolhouse, accessible via State Route 87, offers a glimpse into the early days of education in Arizona Territory.

Built in 1884, the Strawberry Schoolhouse is the oldest standing schoolhouse in Arizona. Its rustic log construction and simple design speak to the pioneering spirit of early settlers in the Strawberry Valley, an area once known for its abundance of wild strawberries and used seasonally by cowboys for grazing livestock.

The schoolhouse's existence is tied to an interesting piece of Arizona history. In the early 1870s, Governor Anson P. K. Safford was shocked to discover that despite having nearly 2,000 school-age children, Arizona Territory had no public schools. His subsequent campaign for education led to the establishment of schools like this one across the territory.

> ### *Fun fact:*
> The Strawberry Schoolhouse operated until 1916, serving generations of local children. Today, it stands as a museum, allowing visitors to step back in time and experience education as it was in Arizona's territorial days.

Visiting the Strawberry Schoolhouse is like taking a journey through time. From the old-fashioned desks to the pot-bellied stove that once kept students warm, every detail tells a story of Arizona's educational past.

Whether you're a history enthusiast, an education professional, or simply curious about Arizona's pioneer days, the Strawberry Schoolhouse offers a unique and enriching experience. It stands as a testament to the importance of education in shaping our communities and our state.

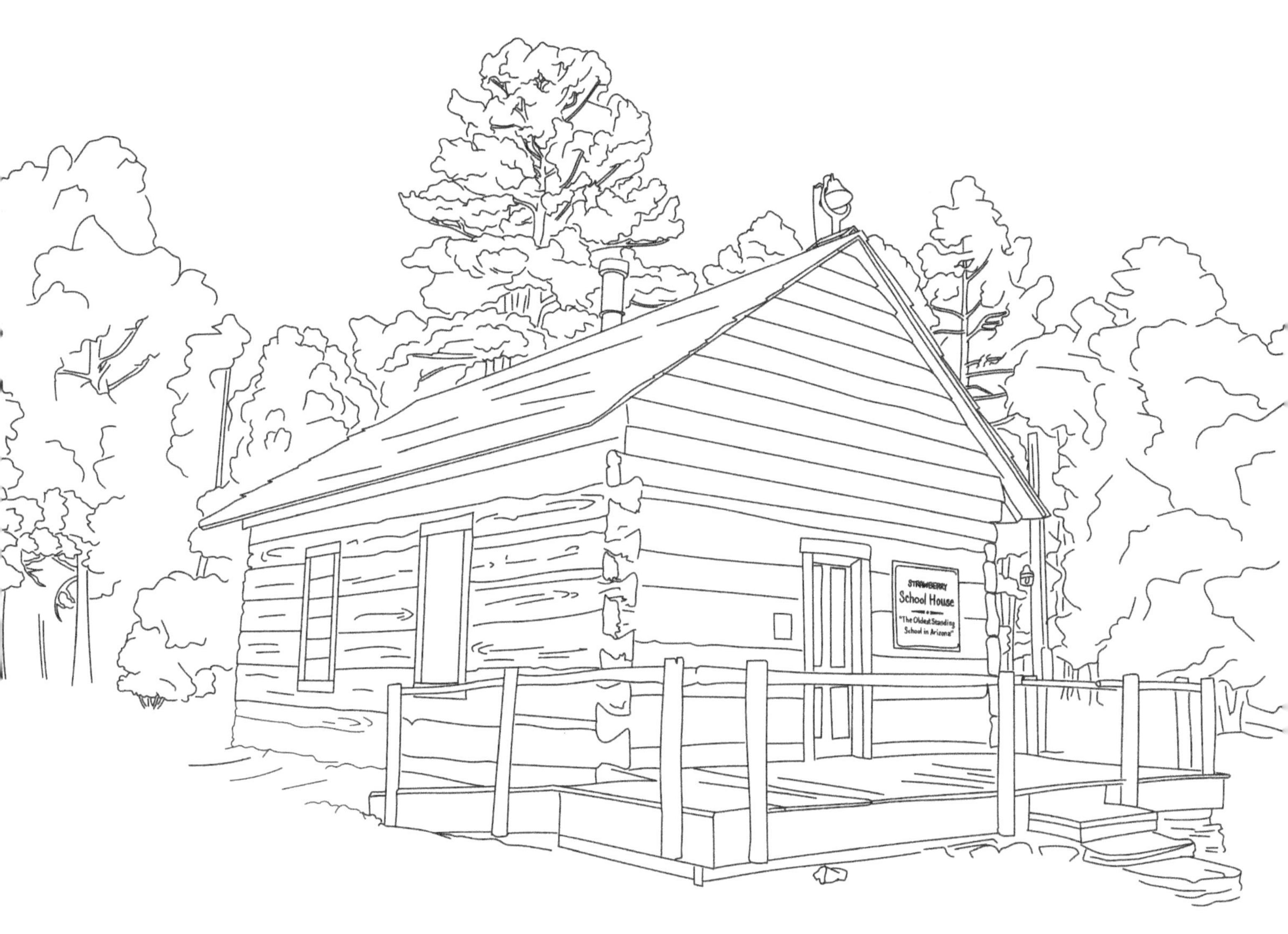
STRAWBERRY
School House
"The Oldest Standing
School in Arizona"

The Julia Randall Historical Rock Building:
A Stone-Hewn Legacy in Payson

Standing proudly in Payson, Arizona, the Julia Randall Historical Rock Building is a testament to the town's rich educational heritage and pioneering spirit. This charming structure, built in 1938, served as Payson's elementary school for many years and now stands as a cherished landmark.

Constructed from local stone, the building's rustic yet sturdy appearance reflects the character of Payson itself - resilient, enduring, and deeply connected to the surrounding landscape. The warm, honey-colored rocks used in its construction were hand-picked from nearby Payson Creek, giving the building a unique connection to the local environment.

Named after Julia Randall, a beloved educator who dedicated over 40 years of her life to teaching Payson's children, the building honors her commitment to education in the Rim Country. Julia Randall's influence on the community went far beyond the classroom, shaping the lives of generations of Payson residents.

The building's architecture is a fine example of Depression-era construction, showcasing the craftsmanship and resourcefulness of the time. Its sturdy stone walls, large windows, and distinctive bell tower have made it an enduring symbol of Payson's commitment to education and community.

Fun fact:

During its construction, many community members, including students, helped gather rocks for the building. This collaborative effort embodies the strong sense of community that has always been a hallmark of Payson.

Today, while no longer serving as a school, the Julia Randall Historical Rock Building continues to play an important role in Payson's community life. It stands as a reminder of the town's history, the importance of education, and the enduring legacy of dedicated educators like Julia Randall.

Whether you're admiring its sturdy stone walls, imagining the generations of students who passed through its doors, or simply appreciating its place in Payson's skyline, the Julia Randall Historical Rock Building offers a tangible connection to Payson's past and its ongoing commitment to education and community.

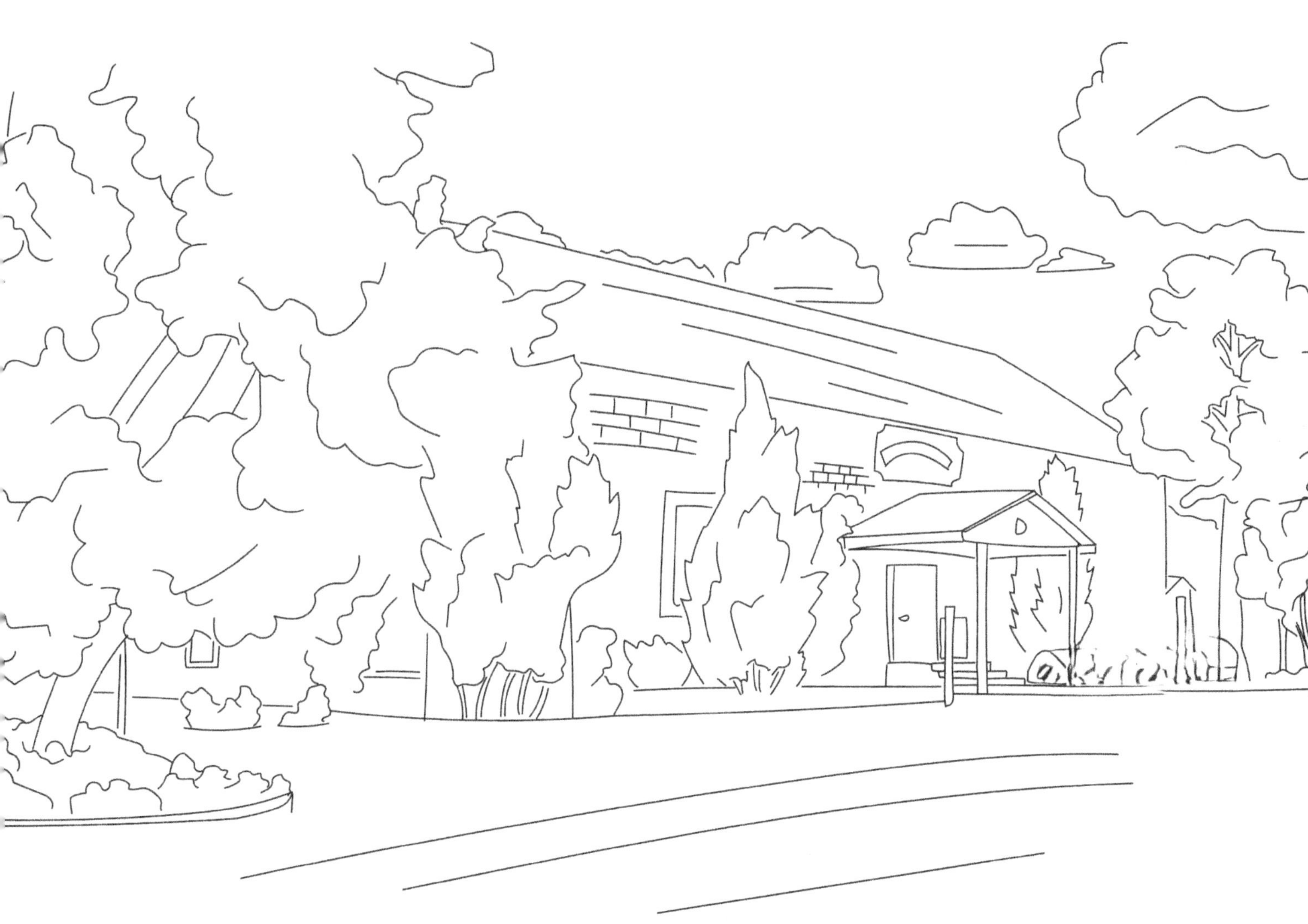

Payson's Seasonal Farmers Market:
A Summer Cornucopia of Local Bounty

From May through September, the heart of Payson comes alive every Saturday morning with the vibrant colors, enticing aromas, and friendly chatter of the local Farmers Market. This seasonal event is a beloved tradition that showcases the best of what Rim Country has to offer during the warm months.

Nestled under the shade of towering pines, the market brings together local farmers, artisans, and food producers from across the region. Stalls brim with an array of fresh, seasonal produce - from crisp early summer greens to late summer's juicy tomatoes and fragrant herbs. The market reflects the diverse microclimates of the area, offering both high-country and desert-grown delights that change as the season progresses.

But it's not just about fruits and vegetables. Visitors can find a wide variety of locally-made goods, including honey from area beekeepers, handcrafted cheeses, freshly baked bread, and colorful bouquets of flowers. Artisans display their wares, from handmade jewelry to rustic wooden crafts, all capturing the spirit of Payson.

The Farmers Market is more than just a place to shop; it's a summer community gathering spot. Neighbors catch up over cups of locally-roasted coffee, families enjoy picnic breakfasts with their market finds, and visitors get a taste of Payson's warm hospitality.

Many of the vendors are happy to share recipes and cooking tips, helping shoppers make the most of their purchases. It's a great place to learn about seasonal eating and sustainable farming practices in Arizona's unique summer climate.

Fun fact:

The market often features live music from local musicians, adding a festive soundtrack to the shopping experience!

The Payson Farmers Market embodies the town's commitment to supporting local businesses and promoting healthy, sustainable living. Whether you're a long-time resident or a summer visitor, a trip to this colorful market offers a delightful way to experience the flavors and friendliness of Payson during the vibrant summer months.

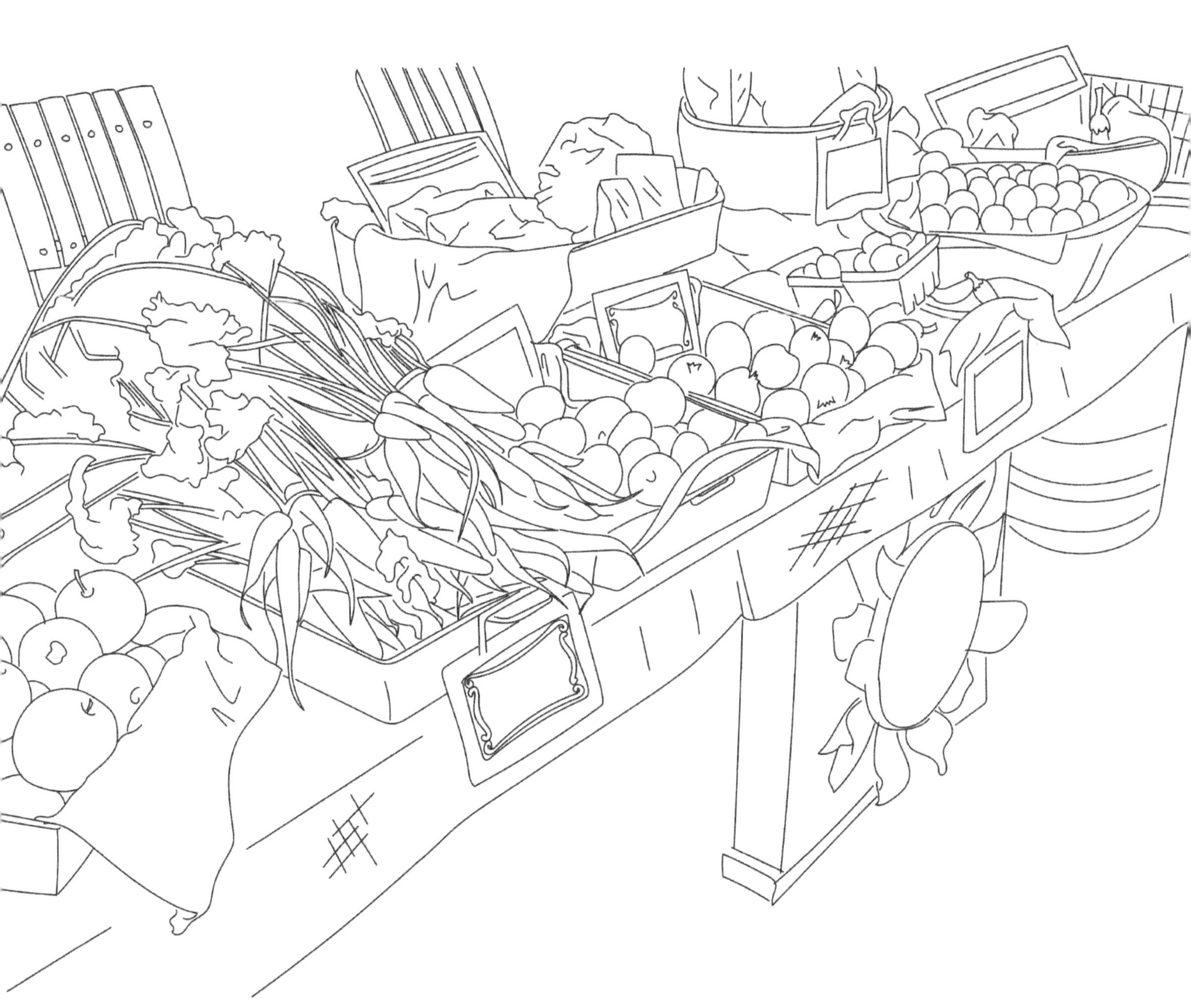

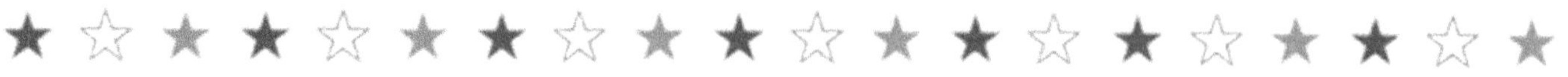

The Randall House in Pine Creek, Arizona

The Randall House, nestled in the charming community of Pine Creek, Arizona, stands as a testament to the area's rich pioneer history. Built in 1881 by the Randall family, this historic homestead offers a glimpse into the lives of early settlers in Arizona's high country.

Constructed with locally-sourced pine logs and featuring a classic frontier design, the Randall House has weathered over a century of Arizona's diverse climate. Its sturdy structure and wide porch are characteristic of the practical yet inviting architecture of the era.

Today, the Randall House serves as a living museum and resturant, showcasing artifacts and stories from Pine Creek's early days. Visitors can explore rooms furnished with period pieces, offering a tangible connection to the past. The house's gardens, maintained in the style of the late 19th century, provide a colorful and fragrant backdrop to this historic gem.

Throughout the years, the Randall House has been a silent witness to the growth and changes in Pine Creek. From its humble beginnings as a family home to its current role as a beloved local landmark, it continues to play an important part in preserving the community's heritage.

Fun fact:

The Randall House is said to have one of the oldest apple trees in Arizona still bearing fruit, planted by the original settlers over 130 years ago!

Whether you're admiring its rustic charm, exploring its historical exhibits, or simply enjoying a peaceful moment on its porch, the Randall House offers a unique opportunity to step back in time and experience a slice of Arizona's pioneer spirit.

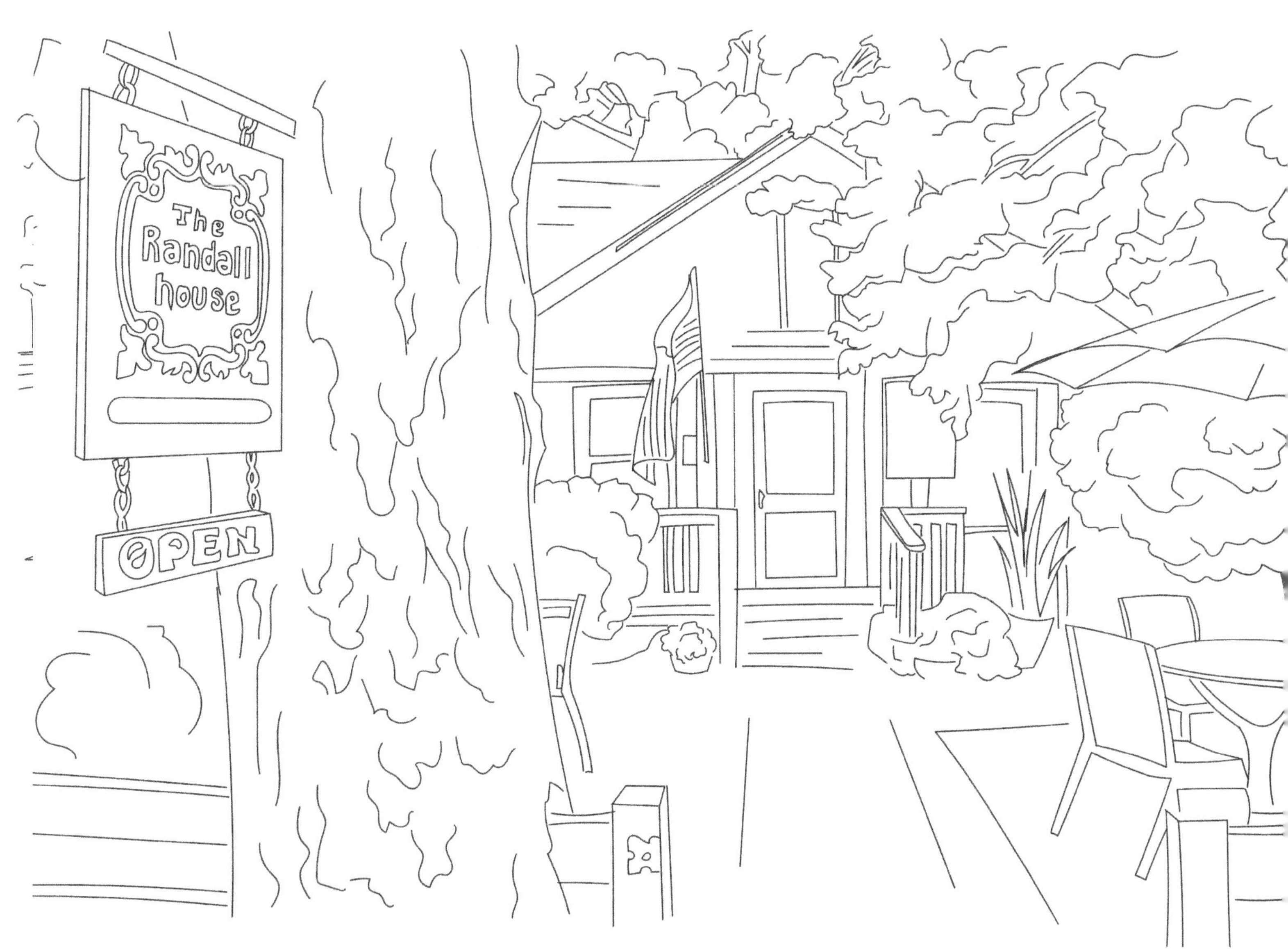

The Randall house
OPEN